The
Development of the Dog

BY THE SAME AUTHOR

NON FICTION

Adventures of an Artisan Hunter
The Complete Jack Russell Terrier
The Complete Lurcher: A Manual
The Cottage at the Edge of the World
Diary of a Hunter
The Fell Terrier
Ferrets
In Pursuit of Coney
Merle: The Start of a Dynasty
Omega
The Sporting Terrier
Tales of a Rat-Hunting Man

FICTION

Trog: A Novel

The Development of the Dog

D. BRIAN PLUMMER

THE BOYDELL PRESS

First published 1995
The Boydell Press, Woodbridge

ISBN 0 85115 637 1

The Boydell Press is an imprint of Boydell & Brewer Ltd
PO Box 9, Woodbridge, Suffolk IP12 3DF, UK
and of Boydell & Brewer Inc.
PO Box 41026, Rochester, NY 14604–4126, USA

British Library Cataloguing-in-Publication Data
Plummer, David Brian
Development of the Dog
I. Title
636.7
ISBN 0–85115–637–1

Printed in Great Britain by
St Edmundsbury Press Ltd, Bury St Edmunds, Suffolk

Contents

The illustration of the bullmastiff on page 46 is reproduced from *The Mastiff and Bullmastiff Handbook* by kind permission of the author D.B. Oliff

I dedicate this book to Pam Harrow – a true friend at all times.

Introduction

I particularly like watching the American comedian George Burns whose act is characterised by raunchy tales of vaudeville, of slightly sleazy downmarket variety acts which were both common and popular in America between the World Wars. Punctuating Burns' anecdotes of incompetent fire-eaters, lascivious fan-dancers and trainers of recalcitrant sea-lions are 'spikey' one-liners epigrammatic in nature and caustic enough to etch their way through steel plate. My favourite one-liner involves one of Burns' stooges eulogising on the sagacity of some mongrel he owns, and goes something like this:

Stooge: 'My dog is just like one of the family.'
Burns: 'Which one?'

Yet there are dog owners who believe their dogs are one of the family and possess not only human faculties and frailties, but to express it yet more succinctly, these owners believe their dogs to be four-footed people, devoid of speech perhaps, but with all the other qualities a person possesses, including conscience, soul and the ability not only to reason but also to evaluate the difference between right and wrong. Yet nothing could be further from the truth and a person's belief that a dog is simply a four-legged human being is the first stage to the production of a team comprising a very wayward dog and a very upset, disturbed and disenchanted dog owner. Dogs in fact, despite the symbiotic relationship they have shared with man for perhaps as long as 100,000 years, are very different from human beings, both in bodily functions and the way their mental processes work. If man has changed the physical and mental state of his oldest ally considerably – and there is little doubt that he has – he has not altered canine make-up enough to narrow the hiatus between the two species to the point where dogs have developed human qualities, frailties or vices.

To the reader who still believes that their dog is simply one of the family, I say which one of the family has a stomach the oxyntic glands of which can secrete acidic juices to digest a long dead crow, without that person suffering from food poisoning? Which member of one's family is capable of scenting the presence of a prey animal half a mile distant? At the risk of seeming indelicate, which of the males of the said family seeks out the privacy of long grass to evacuate its bowels and then strikes the ground with its legs to indicate its presence to sexually available females? Which member of the family is likely to be senile before its fourteenth birthday or will seek to reproduce its own kind before it is one year of age? Which of the females is sexually fertile only twice a year, or which male jealously guards its territory by yet another display of its bodily functions?

Yet people still attempt to seek out similarities between canines and hominids by absurd analogies such as 'One year of a dog's life is equal to seven of a man's' – the most irritating of platitudes any thinking biologist or student of canine behaviour could imagine. Let me debunk this most ludicrous of mathematical formulae by saying that a bitch will be physically ready to mate when it is nine months of age – few young girls of five are capable of conceiving. A small breed male dog will achieve its physical and 'social' peak when it is two years of age – few boys of fourteen are so precocious. The list of differences that make a mockery of this one-to-seven ratio absurd is endless, yet so great is man's desire to seek out similarities in behaviour between dogs and man that this formula is believed by many and repeated by most. It is in fact the differences between the two species that first brought about the union of dog and man and that encouraged the symbiotic relationship that sometimes still exists between the two species.

The Domestication of the Dog

Popular interest in the origins of the domesticated dog began in earnest in Victorian times, though naturalists such as Buffon and Cuvier speculated on the possible antecedents of the various breeds of dogs a century earlier. However, it was in Victorian times that the scientific search for the ancestors of the modern dog began in earnest and popular children's books of the day, disregarding the moralistic tone that characterised literature of the times, related how the children of Ig and Og returned to the caves with wolf cubs, which they persuaded their fond and indulgent parents to allow them to keep. These wolf cubs tamed easily, quickly became the adoring sychophantic creatures we know today, instantly sloughing off their lupine ways to become domesticated dogs. Other writers of children's books, in an attempt to be a shade more realistic, suggested that in times of hardship, when the deer failed to materialise and the wild roots were less abundant, the children tried to prevent the still brutish Ig and Og from devouring the succulent cubs and thus bringing an end to the domestication of the dog.

However, before subjecting such writings to the criticism that not only are such tales a shade 'twee' but that they are highly unscientific and a shade anthropomorphic as well, might I submit that there is perhaps more than a hint of truth in the way these Victorian writers of children's books suggest that the bond between dog and man might have been forged. If Dembeck (*Animals and Man*) is correct, man in particular, and hominoids in general, might be unique among animals in his desire to keep pets of all sorts. In fact it is highly likely that the dog was not the first animal these hominids sought to domesticate.

There is evidence, albeit slight evidence, that Neanderthal man, who may have been one of the ancestors of modern man, kept cave bears in captivity, feeding and tending these huge herbivorous brutes some twice the size of the modern Kodiak grizzly bear on a variety of vegetable foods before ritually stoning the bewildered creatures to death. Other schools of anthropology suggest that these creatures merely shared the labyrinthine caves with these Neanderthals and again, according to Dembeck, were slain as soon as they became numerous enough to be considered as competitors with the hominoids with which they shared these caves.

More curious still is the tale of a giant sloth found walled up in a crevice in a South American cave in which the creature subsequently perished. Carbon datings on the mummified corpse indicated that the creature probably pre-dated the domestication of dogs in the New World, though it would be interesting to hear how such anthropologists explain the origin of the cur dogs described by the Bernal Diaz De Castillo in his account of village life prior to Cortez' conquest of Mexico. If these dogs had accompanied the Amerindian on his migration across the stretch of sea now known as the Bering Straits, then surely the domestication of these dogs occurred in Asia and must predate the domestication and incarceration of the giant sloth, if that creature was ever truly domesticated.

Lorenz in his fascinating but heretical book *Man Meets Dog* suggests that dogs are polyphyletic (derived from more than one species) in origin and both the wolf and the gold jackal (*Canis aureus*) are the ancestors of the dog. Lorenz's thinking is both complex and a shade lateral in nature, for he believes that the more malleable and tractable breeds such as the German shepherd and the collie are derived from the golden jackal, and the more aloof breeds such as the chow chow are descendants of the Palaearctic wolf.

Lorenz's suggestion as to how the bond between man and dog was formed is, however, both interesting and logical. Jackals, which despite their scavenging ways are also capable of hunting live prey, would have haunted the dwellings of early man, feeding on scraps and devouring human faecal matter, thereby keeping the camp sites relatively disease free. Lorenz suggests that these jackals would have sometimes sallied forth with the human hunters and contributed to the capture of the quarry. A symbiotic bond between man and the ancestors of domesticated dogs would have soon been forged when man's better vision and higher intelligence was complemented by the greater speed and scenting power of the early canines which accompanied man – a certain species of wolf would behave in much the same way as the golden jackal. Indeed, Indian wolves are not only less afraid of man than their Palaearctic equivalents, but also more omnivorous and willing to sanitise human middens.

Less tame jackals/wolves/wild dogs would break away from their camp followers, whereas the more tolerant canines would be more successful in obtaining their share of the kills, and hence would more readily perpetuate their kind and also their disposition. Whether or not this domesticating process took many thousands of years to evolve or whether the taming of the wild canines could be accomplished in a man's lifetime is debatable and forthwith the reader must forgive a digression to illustrate how quickly change can be wrought in a species by selective breeding.

Shortly after World War II the traditional table poultry was the Rhode Island Red/Light Sussex first cross, a sex linked hybrid the cock birds of which were predominantly white and the females a dull dowdy brown colour. However, moves were afoot to breed hybrid types of poultry which would in time breed true to type, grow quickly and be far more commercially viable than the traditional meat-bred cross breeds. These hybrids, Ross and Cobb etc. derived in part from Cornish game birds, were quite profitable to rear and hence hatcheries produced hundreds of thousands of these table birds. Certain breeders set eggs, waited the full twenty-one days for the majority of chicks to hatch and promptly sold off the day-olds, keeping the later hatch, the chicks that had taken twenty-two or twenty-three days to leave the shell, as further breeding stock, for they were genetically identical to the birds that were sold as 'day-olds'. Or were they? In a very short period of time, a mere dozen or so generations, it was found that the hatcheries which adopted this process of selection were having to incubate the batches of eggs for twenty-two days to produce a single chick and the majority of the hatch shed their shells after twenty-three days of incubation. Now the colourful jungle fowl *Gallus bankiva*, the ancestor of the domesticated fowl, enjoys an incubation period of twenty-one days and has probably done so for perhaps several million years. Yet in a matter of ten or so generations man, by unintentional selection, has changed the fundamental breeding pattern of a variety of fowl. The notion that evolution proceeds at a slow plodding rate, slowly allowing the organism to make minuscule changes to its form and habits, is illogical and easily disproved. Even Darwin and Haekel were forced to accept that the Porto Santo rabbit was simply a descendant of the domesticated rabbit that had evolved into an entirely new species in a period of less than four hundred years.

Most cynologists reject Lorenz's notion that the jackal was the ancestor of the modern dog, though it is curious that jackals, wolves, dogs and coyotes will mate with each other and produce fertile hybrids, so it is just possible that some jackal blood may well be present in the lineages of some breeds of domesticated dog. However, most cynologists now accept that the wolf is the ancestor of most, if not all, the domesticated breeds of dog.

Yet few are prepared to accept that a single species of wolf gave rise to all breeds of dog. Fiennes and Fiennes (*The Natural History of The Dog*) suggest that if the dog is polyphyletic in origin it is simply descended from various species of wolves. This book suggests that the spitz-type dogs, the German shepherd and all breeds of terrier are descended from the Northern Wolf *Canis lupus* and that the stronger, brachycephalic breeds such as the 'bull breeds' and the numerous mastiff are the descendants of mountain wolves such as the large, powerful broad-headed Tibetan wolf *Canis lupus chanco* or *Canis lupus laniger*, an enormous lumbering wolf which was once the scourge of the caravans which travelled the Silk Road from China to Constantinople. Like Zeuner in *History of Domesticated Animals*, the Fiennes believe that the Arabian wolf, *Canis lupus arabs*, a dolichocephalic type of wolf, frail in physique but fleet of foot, was the ancestor of virtually all the types of sight hound, such as greyhounds, borzois, deerhounds, salukis and wolfhounds.

More curious still is the Fiennes' notion that the dingo, the basenji and the Rhodesian ridgeback are descendants of a similar type of wolf *Canis lupus pallipes*. Zeuner is a little more flexible in his approach and suggests that the numerous breeds of half-wild dingo-type dogs which inhabit Melanesia and Australasia are possibly the true ancestors of all the modern breeds of dogs.

Wolves are certainly not difficult to tame, though they are not so easily trained, one must add. Indeed so easily are wolves domesticated that Lois Crisler in her book *Arctic Wild* (1956) mentions how dog-like wolves become if taken from their natural dam at an early age and hand reared. So easily were the Crisler wolves domesticated that the enigmatic Mrs Crisler destroyed the wolves she had reared from wild young cubs because she could not stand to see what captivity had done to them – a somewhat bizarre solution to her dilemma perhaps.

Lucas in *Pedigree Dog Breeding* (1925) suggests that dogs and foxes will freely hybridise and produce fertile offspring, while Haagerdoorn, in *Animal Breeding* (1952), proposes that breeders of silver foxes – furbearing foxes that are simply domesticated colour forms of the red fox and kept for their splendid pelts – should introduce 'dog genes' into their foxes to give the stock greater immunity to distemper. Prior to production of a suitable vaccine, distemper was the scourge of silver fox breeding establishments for foxes have little immunity to this disease. Lucas's mention of the hybrid is interesting and for months prior to the publication of his book he engaged in a series of letters to *The Field* defending his belief in the fox/dog hybrid. Apparently a vixen kept in the middle of the bustling village of Le Turbie gave birth to a litter of puppies or cubs which Lucas believed had been sired by a dog, for Lucas considered it virtually impossible for the vixen to be served by a visiting male fox, as the animal would have been required to journey far into the town to effect the union.

However, if the reader will permit me to digress once again, a tale might well disprove Lucas's notion as the nature of the sire of the cubs. In 1984 I taught in a congested district of North Walsall near an estate which was heavily populated, with little access to fields or the countryside. In one street lived an interesting character called Platts, who kept a variety of fancy pigeons and semi-exotic livestock. One of his pets was a vixen he had reared from a cub and which was allowed liberty to roam where she pleased. In the spring of 1984 the vixen was obviously pregnant and dug a den under the kennel in which Platts kennelled her. She produced a litter of blue-black cubs which she allowed her owner to handle and which became as tame as the vixen, but the sire of the litter was clearly a male fox who had somehow braved the traffic of the estate to mate with the vixen.

The wolf, the possible ancestor of the domesticated dog

The common red fox, *not* the ancestor of the domesticated dog

There is in fact absolutely no evidence to suggest that foxes will breed with dogs, though I have deliberately force mated vixens to a particularly precocious young male terrier I once owned. The pair mated and tied in much the same manner as dogs though the vixen was decidedly upset by the tie and screamed and cavorted to disengage herself from the male. The union was encouraged some four times until the vixen refused to accept the attentions of the dog and hid when he approached her, but no puppies-cum-cubs resulted from the union. I have met many people who have deliberately attempted this crossbreeding yet have never met anyone who has succeeded in producing a litter from the union of dog and fox. Yet bitches repeatedly seem to produce fox-like puppies which their owners claim to have been sired by a male fox. One such dog, the Nova Scotia ducktolling dog, is extremely fox-like in type and is believed by some to be the result of a union between foxes and gold retrievers. As waterfowl act in a totally predictable manner when a fox appears it is possible that breeders deliberately bred fox-like dogs to secure the waterfowl wild-fowlers are wont to hunt. There is in fact no evidence to suggest that red fox blood was used to create this curiously vulpine-looking breed of retriever.

To disagree with the theories of biologists of the calibre of Lorenz, the Fiennes and Zeuner must seem a heresy, if not a sacrilege, yet I do not believe that the wolf is the ancestor of the domesticated dog or to be more exact that a wolf of some species was the first wild canine to be domesticated. Primitive man balanced on the meat line, a far more slender arête than the breadline – a financial tightrope walked by modern man. Vegetable food can be stored or left in the ground until needed but the diet of the hunter is perishable and short-lived even if sun dried or 'jerked'. Hence man's first hunting companion needed to be not only easily tamed but more malleable and tractable than even the wolves described by Crisler. The remote, distant nature of the wolf would have been little use to primitive, pre-herding man who for thousands of years balanced the tightrope of extinction. If primitive man had cultivated any creature to act as a hunting companion the wolf, no matter what the subspecies, would have hardly been the ideal creature with which man could form a symbiotic relationship. Wolves are recalcitrant by nature and while they might hear the commands uttered by the primitive hunter, they would almost certainly choose to disregard or ignore them unless it pleased the wolf to do otherwise. Lorenz, in *Man Meets Dog*, mentions walks with his chow chow, a breed he considers to be the embodiment of lupine temperament. The chow chow accompanied him on his walks when it chose to do so, but more often than not chose to range abroad and often disregarded Lorenz's commands. Such a creature would have been a hindrance rather than an aid to the primitive hunter, and even the Niam Niam dog, the primitive basenji-like dog of the Congo watershed (supposedly descended from *Canis lupus pallipes*), can be restrained by the human voice. An animal that is to work in conjunction with man must be obedient to man's commands and aware of man's superior 'decision making' intelligence. A more naturally subservient canine than the wolf would have been more suitable for domestication, though it is fairly obvious that by dint of selective breeding a subservient lupine-type canine could be produced in a very short period of time. Yet the wolf would have hardly appeared the most suitable hunting ally for primitive man during the initial stages of its domestication.

What is also interesting is the great antipathy wild wolves display towards domesticated dogs. Early explorers of the mid west of America record that when wolves troubled the camp-sites they were never interested in the hunters assembled there, despite the fur robes early explorers invariably wore. The wolves came to kill and eat the dogs and the majority of tame dogs were in desperate fear of their wild brethren. Berringer, who helped chart the MacKenzie River area in the early part of the century, records his experiences with sixteen MacKenzie River huskies, huge brutes which Hubbard in *Observers Book of Dogs* states are half wolf. Yet these huskies attracted hungry wolves which hung around the camp-sites where the dogs were tethered and sometimes made forays to capture a dog. Berringer records that once when he was remiss about tethering his dogs and three escaped their restraining tie ropes, they stayed close at hand, fearful of the wolves which watched a hundred yards or so away. Even in Europe the smaller *Canis lupus lipus* has always been a menace to domesticated dogs. The studded steel collars sported by mastiffs and bull terriers are in fact somewhat gentler versions of the spiked collars worn by brachycephalic herding dogs as a protection against wolf attacks. Certain Maremma-type sheepdogs still sport these fearsome spiked collars as protection against wolves.

I cannot but feel that Jack London's tales must have influenced the thinking of modern cynologists. London spent a brief period of time in the Yukon and developed at best a casual knowledge of sled dogs and certainly no knowledge of how to handle them. Yet his fascination for the wild canine, the Timber Wolf, knew no bounds. Just as Rousseau saw the noble savage as the embodiment of all man's lost virtues, so London saw the wolf as the most meritorious of canines. With the exception of Buck, the half-breed shepherd/St Bernard canine hero of *Call of the Wild* and the Irish terriers Jerry and Michael brother of Jerry, virtually all London's canine heroes were wolves or wolf-bred dogs. These superdogs were bright, tolerant of man but never subservient to him, primordial and dominant in their own rights yet possessing every canine virtue. Yet it is highly unlikely that London ever saw a wolf-breed dog during his stay in the Yukon. A variety of mongrel draught dogs were used by hauliers delivering goods to the gold fields, dogs ranging from the mongrel mastiff-types bred by Treadwell Walden and dubbed the Chinook, to the traditional Eskimo dogs of Alaska which would later be standardised and referred to as Malamutes. Yet there is no evidence that wolves' blood was ever brought into the draught dog strains. In fact much of London's reference to wolf-bred arctic draught dogs is coloured by his strange preoccupation with wolves rather than any experience he had with lupine-like sled dogs. He was obsessed with the brute nature of man, of man unrefined by civilisation, and to London the wolf epitomised the golden age prior to the refining effects of civilisation. His close associate George Sterling often received letters from London which the author signed 'The Lone Wolf' and his financially ruinous house, which burned down before its completion, was referred to as the Wolf Shack. Wolf Larsen, the powerful and ferocious hero of the *Sea Wolf*, is thought to be a reflection of London's own personality and he entitled his first collection of short stories *The Son of the Wolf*. However, let us return to the subject of the Alaskan malamute.

Malamutes, the most wolf-like of the huskies, dogs which have been deliberately selected over the last hundred years to resemble timber wolves, were supposedly, at least according to legend, bred by chaining in-season husky bitches to the barrens so that wolves would serve them. Yet it is never easy to breed wolf/dog hybrids in captivity and the majority of wolves disdain in-season domesticated bitches even when the bitches are clearly ready to mate.

Raymond Graham Jones, the owner of Southam Zoo, tried for three years to mate his very friendly German shepherd bitch with an equally tame ice cream-addicted timber wolf. In the third year the union was completed and a litter of puppies produced. At first they were friendly but slightly reserved even though they were subjected to great socialising from visitors to the zoo, who saw them as a novelty and played with them at every opportunity. During the year they were bred, dozens of visitors were photographed with these hybrids, but as the cubs-cum-puppies grew older they became more and more nervous, remote and intractable. They were sold via the pages of *Exchange and Mart* for £300 apiece but the fate of these hybrids was scarcely idyllic, possibly due to their nervous disposition. Yet neither the sire nor the dam of these hybrids showed the slightest fear of people.

To return to the subject of the lupine origin of the malamute – the most wolf-like of breeds – one can do little better than relate the tales of Mrs Robert Russell of Sussex, Wisconsin who was at one time President of the Alaskan Malamute Club of America. Mrs Russell not only repudiates the supposed wolf-cross origin of the malamute but is of the opinion that the sale of all wild canines as pets should be prohibited.

Her reasons for her notions are fascinating, as is her tale of the attempts at domesticating the timber wolf Daffney. In 1974 Mrs Russell's husband bought his wife a three week old wolf cub from a wolf farm at Kare Pa, though the owner of the farm, a Mr Lynch, warned the Russells of the danger of wolves to children, Mrs Russell obtained a three week old cub which at this age was totally without fear of humans or dogs and hand-reared the cub for three weeks before placing it in a litter of malamute and Basenji puppies. In this canine pack Daffrey assumed epsilon rank.

The Russells took the cub to various schools and apparently the cub delighted in the attention it received from human beings. However, at four months of age the cub became extraordinarily shy of human attentions (Graham Jones's cubs/puppies also became nervous at about this age), and when people came to visit the litter of mixed puppies (wolf, basenji and malamute) Daffrey hid behind her pen while the others swarmed against the fence to be petted. Despite her constant contact with domesticated dogs no Malamute showed the slightest interest in this she-wolf when she came into season, and avoided coming near her kennel unless they were leashed and persuaded to do so.

Mrs Russell records the tale of a female Malamute bitch puppy, foolish as most first season bitches are, who tried to flirt with a male wolf and nearly lost her leg while doing so. She pushed her paw through the wire of the fence, and the limb was immediately seized by two female wolves within the compound. This of course proves nothing, for terriers become ecstatic when another dog pushes its paw through the wires of their pens and many times I have seen terriers attempt to chew a limb from another dog.

I feel the shyness that wolves manifest as they approach four months of age – and this shyness is apparently common amongst all species of wolf – may well have dissuaded the primitive hunter from seeking an ally with this type of canine. Indian wolves, the most readily tamed of all lupine species, also experience this shyness as the cubs begin to grow to adolescence. Rush, who served in India during the Afghan wars, records that a pair of wolf cubs brought to him by hunters and reared with a boarhound (a mastiff or great Dane composite) were skittishly playful as young cubs and sycophantic towards their dam and owner. Yet as the cubs developed permanent dentition they hid when Rush approached them and refused to feed while he watched them. The camp dogs were distant with, if not hostile to the cubs, which was not surprising when one considers that Rush used this amazing bobbery pack to hunt wolves and other wild canines, and the cubs disappeared back into the forest from whence they came. At least that is what Rush believed, though personally I feel that the antipathy shown them by the camp dogs might more easily explain their disappearance!

Yet it is highly likely that wolves may have played some part in the making of certain breeds of dogs, for wolves will sometimes mate with various breeds of dog and provide fertile hybrids. In fact there are wolf farms (a very loose term, perhaps) in the Mid West of the USA which produce various hybrids for those with an interest in exotic pets. Hybrids ranging from 15:16 wolf/dog to 15:16 dog/wolf are available at these kennels-cum-farms, though what use these hybrids might be is debatable. Apparently the art of breeding the first cross dog/wolf hybrids is to prevent the male wolf developing a monogamous relationship with any dog with which it is intended to breed, and once the male wolf develops polyerotic tendencies the hybrids are easily produced. In defence, these hybrids breeders state that there is a very low incidence of hip dysplasia among the stock they breed – and hip dysplasia seems very prevalent in the German shepherd dog stock these breeders use to produce their crossbreeds. Haagerdoorn mentions a German shepherd dog/ wolf male that was bred as a police dog, but many of Haagerdoorn's statements are regarded with suspicion by modern geneticists. The fact that both Aristotle and Oppian believed dogs regularly coupled with wolves and stated certain hounds were the direct descendants of wolf/dog crosses should be treated with some caution. It is worth noting that Aristotle, whose theories were held in great esteem for a thousand years, believed certain dogs were the result of unions between tigers and dogs (certain mastiffs are still referred to as being of a tiger brindle colouring), and to breed these ferocious tiger hybrids in-season bitches would be tied in forests to be served by passing tigers. The outcome of such a meeting would be both predictable and unpleasant.

The notion that wolf blood was introduced into various strains of sled dog to increase stamina and endurance is also questionable. When George Attla, the world sled dog champion, was once asked about wolf hybrids supposedly bred by Alaskan Indians, he answered that he had never seen one, but had heard of an Indian who reputedly harnessed pure-bred wolves and ran them as sled dogs. They were certainly inferior to the traditional sled dogs but, once again according to Attla, supposedly ran better by night. Yet wolves are renowned for their stamina, though possibly their reputation for endurance is due to their curious loping gait rather than any constitutional peculiarities.

Lopez, in *Of Wolves and Man*, records a tale of an Eskimo hunter who sighted a wolf and desired its pelt. He found that he had left his rifle at home and so determined to run the wolf to a state of exhaustion with his snow mobile, a piece of equipment that seems to have replaced the sled dog in the lives of the modern Eskimo. He ran the wolf for twelve miles at a speed of between fifteen and thirty miles an hour, after which the wolf resorted to a trot to escape capture and continued at this pace for a further four miles before slowing to a walk. Four miles later the exhausted wolf collapsed and was clubbed to death.

Indeed the endurance of the wolf may well have been its salvation in a medieval Europe which was totally antipathetic to him. The *Livre de Chase*, written some time between 1387 and 1390, records how demoralising a wolf hunt could be to the gamest of hounds, that would run themselves into a state of exhaustion yet fail to catch a trotting wolf. It is believed by many that the rough-coated, savage-tempered Welsh hounds, slower and less elegant than the English fox hound, were originally used to hunt wolves, engaging them in a grinding war of attrition before denning or killing them. Yet such hunting was seldom a suitable way of catching wolves. The wolf hounds of Flixton, Stackston and Folkstone, which were some of the ancestors of the modern coursing and track greyhounds, were large, coarse-coated dogs similar to the deerhound of the eighteenth century perhaps, and responsible for the extinction of the last of the English wolves. They were run in conjunction with motley packs of scenting hounds which drove the wolves into clearings where the wolf hounds were slipped at them. Tolstoy, in *War and Peace*, records a similar type of hunting, but in this tale borzois take the place of the English wolf hounds. Few dogs are capable of running down a wolf once it has distanced itself from its pursuers and has assumed its curious loping pace.

Despite London's tales of in-season bitches chained in the snow to attract the amorous attentions of wolves to produce puppies which would grow to become the strongest of sled dogs, there is no evidence that either Eskimo or Indian sled dog 'mushers' ever engaged in this practice. Lopez, in *Wolves and Man*, records that the Amerindian saw little relationship between wolves and dogs and treated them as entirely different species and never 'confused' the two canines. Lopez states that any hybrids between wolves and camp dogs were invariably dangerous and headstrong and unsuitable for camp life, for the Amerindian was pragmatic enough to reject the Europeans' passion for keeping useless and dangerous exotica. Neither did the Eskimo consider dogs and wolves to be forms of the same species. Wolves were credited with souls and treated with a strange respect, even when they fell victims of Eskimo traps and spears. Sled dogs, no matter how wolf-like they appeared to the Europeans who first investigated them, were considered beasts of burden to be used, abused, sometimes eaten and subjected to any indignity. There is in fact little to suggest that either Amerindians or Eskimos ever chained in-season bitches in the snows to mate with wolves (they would like as not be regarded as food rather than mates by wandering, monogamous male wolves), or that the said indigenous American races believed that wolves would willingly and frequently couple with dogs. Lopez cleverly summarised the Crow Indians' opinion of the relationship between dog and wolf within an Aesop-like fable which tells of a conversation between a dog and a wolf, in which the wolf despises the subservient behaviour of the dog despite the relatively easy life of the camp cur. Fables concerning wild and tame animals conversing on the merits and disadvantages of their lots are abundant the world over, and Jung considers these tales to be an indication that man somehow regretted the abandonment of the hunter-gatherer existence he traded for a settled lifestyle.

Strangely enough, despite the fact that the wolf has always enjoyed the reputation of being a rapacious stock killer, there is little evidence to suggest that wolves were ever the formidable man-eaters of legend. Ernest Thompson Seton believes that before the advent of guns, powerful bows and suitable poisons, wolves may have regarded man as a prey species – particularly in the winter months when food would have been scarce and primitive man clad in animal furs may have precipitated an attack from wolves. Corbett believes the evil stench exuded by human beings may well have deterred all but the most desperate of predators and it is certainly true that human carcasses are frequently ignored by scavengers until putrefaction has removed most of the undesirable stench animals associate with live human beings.

Stephanson, in his book *Adventures in Error*, questions as to whether wolves have ever been a danger to man – though pre-Promethean man may have certainly been regarded as a prey species by wolves despite his objectionable scent. Stephanson went to considerable trouble to check on every report of a wolf attacking a man between the years 1923–1936 and found not a single instance of a healthy wolf ever attacking a child, let alone an adult. Cases of wolf attacks when properly investigated proved to be instances where the wolves were rabid and even a rabid cat will attack with the ferocity of a tiger. Curiously Pasteur's first patient during his research into rabies was Joseph Meister, a young boy who had been the victim of an attack by what Meister's mother believed to be a rabid wolf.

Stephanson's report caused considerable interest and some disbelief – the same interest and disbelief that has been engendered by the Aberdeen University report that foxes are not a danger to lambs. Thus it was that James Curran, editor of the Ontario newspaper *Daily Star*, offered a reward of $100 to anyone who could substantiate an account of a wolf attacking a human being. Curran died several years later, but his reward money, while it gave his paper great publicity, went unclaimed.

Concerning the subject of wolves and wolf/dog hybrids it would be expedient to include at least an account of the terrible Beasts of Gevaudan and the bobtailed wolf Corto, both of which are well documented. In the midsummer of 1764 a series of strange deaths were reported in the Cevennes mountains in the south-central area of France. At first children were found killed and badly mutilated. Indeed, most of the victims of these attacks were children under the age of twelve, but tales of horsemen unseated from their steeds and subsequently disembowelled were also common. Curiously the tale of a priest thrown by his mule, which continued to graze near the spot where its rider was half eaten, attracted the greatest interest amongst the very superstitious peasantry who credited the predators with some diabolic motives.

A large sum of money was offered for anyone who would trail the creatures which apparently left bloody footprints some twice the size of those made by wolves and these tales, plus the large reward offered for the capture of the beasts, attracted armies of hunters from all over Europe. Yet despite the fact that the forests were beaten and driven by hounds no trace of the creatures was seen, though hundreds of small wolves and feral dogs were slain by the hunters who combed the Cevennes. However, each time the *battues* ceased yet another spate of killings took place and there were few who doubted the supernatural nature of the killers. Eventually an elderly hunter Antoine de Bauterne, who had lived in the district for several years, shot what appeared to be an oddly-coloured male wolf, a colossal brute which stood thirty-two inches at the shoulder and measured sixty-seven inches from nose to tail, or larger than any wolf ever seen in Europe. In June 1767 a female, not quite as large but equally oddly coloured, was shot and the killings promptly ceased.

C.H.D. Clarke, who published an account of the events in 1971, concludes both creatures were dog/wolf hybrids and it is interesting to note that both the animals were very similar to some of the first cross wolf/German shepherd hybrids bred at many of the wolf farms in the USA – and considered by the President of the Malamute Club of America to be very dangerous animals to keep – particularly as the majority of people who would wish to own such creatures would make totally unsuitable owners of such beasts.

Yet there is a considerable market for these cross breeds (particularly those with a more lupine appearance) in Europe. Few Russian films seem complete without scenes where a pack of savage wolves attack a horse-drawn troika in which is travelling a fur-clad beautiful woman. Yet to secure such film footage using authentic wolves would be virtually impossible and the sight of animals which are clearly not wolves engaged in a conflict with the horses would render the film unrealistic. Indeed, the film *The Trap* was ruined for many viewers by the fact that the animals which were required to attack and mutilate Oliver Reed were quite obviously German shepherd dogs, two of which sported long coats!

In order to create greater authenticity, Eastern Bloc film companies employ the services of two animal tamers cum big game hunters called the Sigethy Brothers, of Gondollo, Hungary to produce wolf-like dogs. These are produced by mating a monogamous wolf with a German shepherd bitch and the progeny are virtually identical with the description of the Beast of Gevaudan, being huge wolf-grey beasts with fawn legs and wolflike heads. These hybrids are incredibly dangerous, as they have lost the fear of man that is present in wolves and need to be controlled by gun, whip or heavy stick.

An even greater enigma is the tale of the wolf Corto or Courtaud which in 1447 appeared at the walls of Paris and virtually held the city to siege. Courtaud was bob-tailed, perhaps as a result of an accident, or quite possibly because the animal had been docked. Together with ten or twelve other wolves, Courtaud attacked any domestic animals which were being driven to Paris, stalking the prey animals from the brambles that grew along the road into Paris. In 1450, during a particular sharp fall in temperature, the pack found their way into the city via a breach in the wall and in an orgy of slaughter apparently slew and ate forty people. Eventually the Mayor of Paris declared war on the pack and lured them into a cul-de-sac bated with slaughtered and disembowelled cattle. Here they were shot, stoned and speared to death. The wolves apparently lived in caves in a district now known as the Louvre – 'the cave of wolves' – though the lineage of the wolf Courtaud has long been debated and he is generally considered to be a hybrid dog/wolf which would explain the bobtail, for it was common to dock the tails of country curs – hence the expression 'to curtail'.

However, there is little indication that wolves have ever preyed on human beings, and quite considerable evidence to substantiate tales of children being suckled by wolves. The tale of Romulus and Remus, the supposed founders of Rome, is well-known. The pair were supposedly the sons of a vestal virgin Ilea Rhea, or Silvia, and were sired by the god Mars who violated the priestess. The sons were taken to the wilderness and left to perish but were rescued by a suckling she-wolf who reared the twins until a swineherd called Faustulus found them and brought them up as his own sons.

Lopez, in *Wolves and Men*, offers a fascinating explanation of the legend. He suggests that Faustulus reared the children and that the swineherd's wife was a loose woman. The Latin slang for a cheap prostitute and a she-wolf is 'lupa' so it is possible, at least according to Lopez, that the twins were reared in a bordello rather than the wilderness. Yet legend aside, there is some considerable evidence to suggest that wolves will sometimes adopt and rear suckling children, though it is also likely that wild predators would be more likely to devour rather than foster infants they found unprotected.

Rousseau, who believed that man lost not only much of his freedom but also his fundamental dignity when he embraced civilisation, was greatly interested in the subject of children who were said to have been reared by wild animals. He wrote copiously on the wolf-child of Hesse, a male who was apparently reared by a she-wolf and possessed qualities manifested by wild beasts, and having a moral attitude far removed from the perfidious nature which Rousseau considered characterised man. The wolf-boy of Hesse is certainly not the only example of children reared by wolves in Europe, though the child's development is remarkably similar to the legendary wolf-man of the Transoxianic knot who became the founder of the Seljuk Turkish nation. Linnaeus, who sought to classify all aspects of flora and fauna, categorised some nine children reared by sheep, bears, dogs, cows and pigs as *homo ferus*, wild man, in 1758 and he chose to ignore numerous tales of such children which he failed to substantiate with hard evidence. There is little doubt that

Kipling's Mowgli, the child reared by wolves, hero of *The Jungle Book*, was inspired by numerous tales the author had heard during his stay in India. Indeed, Kipling's father John Lockwood Kipling, published a book called *Beast and Man in India* in 1891. Tales of children appearing on the outskirts of villages in the company of wolves foraging in the rubbish, or attacking sheep and goats alongside their lupine companions, were commonly heard in India at the turn of the twentieth century. When captured the man-children ate raw meat, avoided bright light, were nocturnal or carpuscular in habits and snarled, lifting their lips to expose teeth and gums to indicate their displeasure. Yet while Kipling heard many of these tales he was never able to substantiate them with hard evidence and his *Jungle Book* hero strides back and forth into the worlds of man and beast with amazing alacrity.

Lopez, however, credits such tales with a little substance and quotes the strange tale of the Dent Wolf Girl. In May 1835 a child was born to Mollie Pertul Dent in a cabin near Dent's River, Texas, and the father riding for help was killed by a thunderstorm. The mother and child were never found and the rescuers believed that wolves had devoured them.

Some ten years later a young Mexican boy living near San Phillipe Springs reported a naked girl, long hair covering her features, attacking a herd of goats in the company of several wolves and this tale, coupled with reports of Apache scouts who had seen a child's footprints mingling with the pad marks of wolves, triggered off a hunt by local homesteaders. After three days of beating the countryside the girl was cornered in a canyon in the company of a wolf which attacked the party when the group attempted to capture the girl.

The girl was taken to a nearby ranch and incarcerated in a room, the doors of which had been locked and bolted, but the child began to howl piteously after the manner of a wolf and attracted packs of wolves, which lay about the perimeter of the ranch house 'spooking' the horses and frightening the livestock. In the subsequent confusion the girl managed to escape and some seven years later was reported playing on a sandbar on the Rio Grande by a surveying party from El Paso. She was never seen again after this date.

More amazing still is the tale of the wolf-children Amala and Kamala whose story gave the world press much copy in the mid and late 1920s. On 17 October 1920 the Reverend J.A.L. Singh, who ran the orphanage at Midnapore in India, heard curious tales of ghost dwarfs living in the anthills just outside the village of Godamuri. These ghost dwarfs were said to live with wolves and to imitate the ways of the smaller Indian wolf and, because the natives near to Godamuri were terrified of the ghost dwarfs, Singh was forced to bring in outside help to excavate the anthill.

As the diggers began to delve into the fine soil that constituted the anthill, two male wolves bolted and attempted to escape, but the she-wolf attacked the diggers with such ferocity that she had to be shot. Further into the mound the diggers came upon a chamber in which two wolf-cubs and two small children were entwined in what Riddle refers to as a 'monkey ball' – where both parties assume a foetal position induced by sheer terror and intertwine their arms and legs. Quite suddenly both parties would untangle from the monkey ball and make furious sallies at the diggers, before retreating once more into the tangle of arms and legs. The children and the cubs were withdrawn from the chamber in the anthill and from then on the Reverend Singh's part in the tale becomes somewhat confused. It appears that Singh lost control of the children for some five days, during which time they were kept in a cage so small they were unable to stand and at the end of this time they were so weak they could scarcely lap water. Singh's diary states that they had been sold in the marketplace of Godamuri to a man who collected curios. However, on 4 November of the year of their capture, they arrived at Singh's orphanage at Godamuri. Singh christened the younger child Amala and estimated her age to be perhaps eighteen months. Amala was never a healthy child, which considering her ordeal in the days prior to the orphanage is understandable, and she died of uraemic poisoning a year later.

The older child Kamala lived until she was perhaps seventeen – Singh estimated her age as eight at the time of her capture. Kamala sucked meat, avoided human beings but enjoyed cordial relationships with dogs. She avoided bright lights after the manner of wolves and sought out raw and putrid meat by scent. Kamala was once observed devouring the putrid entrails of a fowl and both children took some time to learn to walk upright – indeed it is believed that man's tendency to walk upright has to be learned or copied and may not be entirely instinctive.

Unlike an Edgar Rice Burroughs hero, neither child learned to speak or to communicate with people and while this tale was disbelieved by many scientists, the reporter Charles McClean eventually sought out evidence to substantiate Singh's strange tale and published his findings in the book *Wolf Children* in 1977.

That both children were autistic seems highly likely – indeed children at the Sonia Shankman clinic have been observed behaving in the same manner as the Godamuri children, but the difference in the ages of the children would be difficult to explain. The practice of abandoning children observed to be peculiar, or possibly mentally defective, is not unknown in many communities which are impoverished and unable to provide for children with physical or mental difficulties. Whether the she-wolf found both children abandoned some six years apart and fostered each in turn, or whether both children were siblings who were abandoned once their mother came to believe she was afflicted with some curse that ensured she produced such abnormal offspring, is debated by many psychologists.

It is, however, interesting to note that the distress cries of certain mammals attract and often disturb mammals of an entirely different species. The family pet dog will often become very excited and disturbed by the distress cries of a new baby. Conversely the bleat of a puppy left in a new house for the first night after separation from its dam and siblings will often distress its owner so much that the owner will take the puppy to bed – thereby sowing the seeds of further problems, one should add. Some owners still become so upset with the persistent bleating of a newly purchased puppy, that after a night of listening to the pitiful whining of the confused whelp they return the dog to the breeder the very next morning.

I have always considered that the reaction of the dog to the new baby and the reaction of the owner to the newly purchased puppy, or rather the bleat of the puppy, to be the result of some symbiotic relationship that has developed between dog and man – a relationship that has taken tens of thousands of years to develop. This, however, would not explain why a wolf (which had not experienced domestication or experienced much contact with man other than to enjoy a predator/prey relationship) should be excited by the bleat of an abandoned child and seek to adopt and rear the child.

I now must beg the reader's forgiveness for the anecdote I am about to relate which may possibly explain why a creature might seek to adopt the young of the species to which it is antipathetic or regards as prey. It is a well-known fact that ferrets will kill and eat rats and enjoy young ratlings – naked and blind rats of a week or so of age. In days long gone, thankfully, it was a common practice of rodent operatives to throw nests of live ratlings for ferrets to eat, and as ferrets are often wont to carry their food into the darkness of a sleeping box to feed, some jills carried ratlings into the boxes where they were feeding their own ferret kittens. Sometimes the bleat of a ratling, quite unlike the distress cry of a baby mustelid, would upset a jill so much that she would carry the young rat to her own nest and, once its scent had mingled with that of her own young, suckle and rear the rat.

Prior to the passing of the 1911 Protection of Animals Act, it was not uncommon to find sideshows accompanying travelling fairs in which a ferret nursing her kittens and a ratling were on display. In the autumn when the kittens were reasonably mature and capable of killing rats, this sideshow became more macabre for it was common to see the showman tip in wild rats which both the ferrets and the fostered ratling attacked, dismembered and ate. There is ample proof that these acts were commonly staged around the Walsall area at the turn of the century, but after the prosecution of Manship of the Ship Inn, Leicester in 1912, acts involving the killing of captured rats ceased.

Despite the tales of wolves fostering orphaned and abandoned children and the resemblance of wolves to dogs, there is some evidence to suggest that the wolf is not the ancestor of the domesticated dog, or not the ancestor of the first domesticated dog to be more exact. Personally, I am inclined to favour the notions of certain Victorian writers who were influenced by the findings of Alfred Russell Wallace (1823–1913), who believed that the dingo, or perhaps an ancestor of the dingo, is also the ancestor of the modern domesticated dog.

It is possible to believe that a species of wild dog teetering perhaps on the brink of extinction stayed close to the encampments of man, scavenging on the camp wastes and just occasionally killing medium-sized prey species – deer, for example. An alliance between the two species could possibly be effected simply because the dog contributed nose and speed of movement to the union, while man, because he walked upright, was able to see far greater distances and because of his superior intelligence was able to devise complex hunting techniques to facilitate the capture of faster and stronger prey species. Dingoes are more readily tamed than wolves, possibly because they are feral dogs and possibly because early man, who domesticated the first ancestors of the dingo, would have selected tamer animals to perpetuate a species which later took to a feral lifestyle. Lorenz found the dingo he kept similar in many ways to the domesticated dogs, but it was never as easily disciplined as were his own domesticated canines. It was once said that true dingoes could never really be broken to stock and could never be trusted with sheep.

Before proceeding further the reader must now forgive me another digression to explain a point. The German zoologist Heck, in his explorations into the nature and type of the extinct bovine, the Auroch, allowed every type of primitive cattle – the Spanish fighting bull, the Highland cattle, and the aggressive Chillingham White cattle, together with the almost feral Corsican cattle – to breed indiscriminately in a large park. In a very short period of time he produced animals which were indistinguishable from the wild auroch (*bos primagenus*) which were believed to be the ancestors of domesticated cattle. These he dubbed Aurochsen, and they not only resembled the wild auroch which apparently became extinct in the seventeenth century, but were 'fierce, temperamental and extremely agile'. Thus Heck concluded that if domesticates were allowed to breed indiscriminately, and not subject to the selective breeding schemes employed by man since earliest times, there was a tendency for domesticates to revert to a type that resembled their wild ancestors. Heck's Aurochsen resembled not only the drawings of the last aurochs by Topsill but the drawings of primitive cattle found in cave paintings throughout Europe.

Likewise domesticated barnyard fowl, allowed to breed indiscriminately, will sometimes revert to specimens resembling the primitive black-red jungle fowl (*Gallus bankiva*) and some of the older breeds of English farmyard poultry – the Old English Pheasant fowl or the Derbyshire red cap – are coloured very similarly to the primitive stock from which all domesticated poultry are supposedly descended.

I believe I have now paved the way to advance, if not prove, my premise. Dogs allowed to roam the streets, allowed to breed indiscriminately as they have often been allowed to do in certain cities, much to the chagrin of local residents, will often revert to animals which closely resemble dingoes in shape, height and coat. Dogs abandoned on certain islands – for example Juan Fernandez, the Robinson Crusoe island of Alexander Selkirk – also tended to revert to this primitive type, though many of the dogs found on Juan Fernandez were greyhounds in type and considerably taller than dingoes, which measure perhaps 22 to 24 inches at the shoulder. Darwin, too, was of the opinion that the only way to determine the appearance of the ancestor of the wild dog was to allow a great many types of dog to breed indiscriminately and to observe which type these mongrelised dogs reverted to.

Those opposed to the notion that the dingo or dingo-like wild dog is the ancestor, or one of the ancestors of, all domesticated dogs are quick to point out that dingoes do not bark in the manner of most dogs, but barking may well be a characteristic that domestication has brought about.

To those not conversant with the dingo, the animal is the wild dog of Australia, a yellow or reddish-brown dog that apart from man is the only indigenous Australian mammal that is not marsupial – pouch-bearing. However, the term 'indigenous' is questioned by many who believe that perhaps dingoes were brought to Australia by the Aborigines who crossed the narrow straits separating the East Indies from Australia in dug-out boats.

The theory that the dingo was brought to Australia by migrating man, whether or not the Aborigine we know today effected the importation, is open to question. Riddle, in *The Wild Dogs*, mentions that dingo bones have been excavated from strata containing the bones of long extinct marsupials, pouched replicas of some of the mammals of other continents: the Thylacoleo, a lion-sized predator; Polarchestes, a giant kangaroo; Euryzygoma, an enormous hippopotamus-like beast, all creatures which survived the late Prehistoric Ice Age but died out when the continent began to warm up again. Thus the dingo may well have existed in Australia long before the Aborigine, or the Aborigine we know today, arrived on the continent. However, it is possible that the Aborigine was not the first indigenous Australian race and some believe that the dingo may well have been brought to the continent by a long extinct race which made the crossing long before the modern Aborigines arrived in Northern Australia. Leakey and Lewin in *Origin* go yet one stage further and suggest that there is no good reason why man may not have migrated to Australia 20,000 years ago, and if he had it is unlikely that the migrants would have been the Aborigines encountered by Captain Cook and other early explorers of the continent. Leakey and Lewin suggest that a land bridge existed between New Guinea and Australia and that some form of primitive man migrated along this bridge accompanied, perhaps in the most loose sense of the word, by the dingo. Not everyone shares Riddle's notions concerning the dingo. The Dingo Study Foundation is attempting to show that the dingo is not really a feral dog, but a species of small wolf, a variety of the Asian wolf *Canis lupus pallipes*, but there seems to be little evidence to support this notion, for dingoes are decidedly more dog-like rather than lupine, and like the domesticated dog have a gestation period of sixty-three days, though they tend to breed only once a year.

Dingoes readily mate with domesticated dogs and produce fertile hybrids. Indeed, during the 1960s the press obtained considerable copy when certain farmers lobbied for stopping the importation of more German shepherd dogs to the continent. Urban dog keepers who tired of their pets were wont to release them in the mountains in the eastern strip and it was found that hybrid German shepherd dogs/dingoes became terrible sheep killers.

Other breeders have supposedly utilised the dingo's natural attributes to produce new breeds of domesticated dogs. It is said that a drover called Timmins found that the Smithfield-type collies imported from Norfolk, England, were not tough enough to drive the half-wild cattle, so he mated these Smithfields (a loose term to describe some of the leggy collies which used to drive mixed flocks along the British droving routes) to dingoes and produced what was to become known as the 'Timmins' biters' – dogs which worked 'tight' to the cattle and used teeth to move recalcitrant animals. Whether Timmins deliberately introduced dingo blood into these strains of herding dog is debatable, and many suggest that these biters were the result of an accidental union between a Smithfield collie and a wild dingo. Further amelioration of the Timmins' biter produced that curious enigma the Australian cattle dog.

Thus the various theories concerning the origin of the modern dog, and now perhaps it is expedient to refer to Fiennes and Fiennes' classification of dogs to explore the fundamental differences between the various breeds of domesticated canids.

Of Dogs and Men

Personally I have great doubts about Fiennes and Fiennes' theory that all the breeds of dog are simply domesticated wolves to which a dash of dingo-type dog or perhaps jackal, or even some extinct species of wild dog, has been added, but their classification is a convenient one so I shall not hesitate to use it to explain the personality traits of the breed types the reader is likely to encounter.

Fiennes and Fiennes classify dogdom into four main groups:

The Northern group – derived almost exclusively from the Palaearctic wolf *Canus lupus lipus*.

The Mastiff group – apparently bred from the Tibetan wolf *Canis lupus chanco* or *laniger*.

The Greyhound group – supposedly bred from an ancestor of the pale-footed Asian wolf, a very lithe and athletic lupine species, or as Zeuner in *History of Domesticated Animals* believes, the desert wolf of Arabia *Canis lupus arabs*.

The Dingo group – again descended from the pale-footed Asian wolf *Canis lupus pallipes*.

The Northern group includes the great variety of northern American and Asian sled dogs which certainly bear a strong resemblance to the wolf, and may well have some wolf blood in their make-up. However, while the northern wolf has a slender, straight tail, similar in type to the tail carried by the modern German shepherd dog, the majority of the sled dogs sport curled or Spitz tails. The Fiennes are quick to explain that this tail may well have been inherited from the dingo type dogs brought north by the migrating Finno Ugrian tribes which apparently were driven north when their homes in the Volga region of Russia were invaded or became overcrowded. This I feel is a totally unsatisfactory explanation of the curious chordal structure of the Spitz breeds, though it is possible that these tribes brought these dogs with them on their migration north, and there may have been some addition of wolf blood to the mix that had already been subjected to many generations of domestication long before the Finno Ugrian migration. Conversely, it is amazing how breeds of animals will, without the help of the selective breeding programme imposed by man, acquire characteristics which suit the climatic zone to which they have been transported. Hence, dingo-like dogs would soon develop features that were tailored to meet the harsh conditions of the Arctic, and may also develop features similar to those manifested by the Palaearctic wolf which is indigenous in the hostile climate of the arctic. Thick fur, slanting eyes (capable of resisting the drying effect of constant winds and the glare of sunlight on snow) and the loping gait sported by the arctic wolf would have suited an animal that was used to haul light or moderately heavy burdens for great distances over snow. Thus it is likely that the sled dogs would acquire wolf-like features to adapt to their environment.

The nature of sled dogs is usually determined by the life-style of their owners. Sled dogs developed by races which obtain a living simply from hunting – malamutes, Siberian huskies, Eskimo dogs – are usually very difficult to train to accept the presence of other domesticates. The Siberian husky is a notorious sheep killer and I know of few who have managed to keep a cat in a house where Siberian huskies are also kept. Sled dog breeds developed by races who augment their hunting existence with reindeer herding – the Samoyeds – are usually more easily accustomed to the presence of stock, quite simply because a dog that is naturally hostile to livestock would enjoy a very brief life in a herder/hunter society.

Likewise, breeds of sled dogs developed by hunting tribes which had not yet embraced other forms of livestock husbandry are usually recalcitrant, untrustworthy and difficult animals to control or train. Herding tribes would need an animal that would not only be used for draught work and hunting, but would also be capable of herding livestock. Hence the Samoyed is more easily trained, is less recalcitrant and infinitely more controllable than its Chuchi cousin, the Siberian husky, which must be one of the most difficult dogs to train to adapt to the life-style enjoyed by a civilised family.

At this stage it is expedient to mention the Alaskan husky to illustrate a point. In the later years of the nineteenth century gold had been found in the Yukon and prospectors, inspired by the great wealth that had resulted from the discovery of gold in California in 1849, flocked north to seek their fortunes in the hostile regions of Alaska and North West Canada. Those who had little notion of the rigours of the land took horses with them to travel to the gold field. Their horses floundered in the mud of the arctic summers, sinking in quagmires made by the passage of other draught animals, or froze to death in the awful temperatures of the arctic winters. Yukon and Alaska were indeed countries which were ill-suited to the use of horses!

Earlier prospectors and trappers had noted how the local Indian and Eskimo tribes had harnessed wolf-like dogs to transport goods and hence the local huskies were eagerly bought up by the first of the prospectors to arrive from the south. However, the local dog 'mushers' were unable to

The Siberian husky

supply the dogs needed by the rush of prospectors, who arrived in thousands at Anchorage, Alaska and trekked to the gold-fields. Hence a host of southern dogs, animals apparently ill-suited to the rigours of the arctic, were snapped up by dog breeders, swiftly broken to harness and driven north to the gold-fields. London, in his book *The Call of the Wild*, paints a dismal picture of hosts of unhappy setters and pointers shivering in front of sleds on the way to the Yukon, but London was woefully wrong. Many of the very best sled dogs were setters and pointers which not only hauled large weights, but were faster and more tractable than the native dogs. Newfoundland and mastiff-type dogs also proved popular and Treadwell Waldren, one of the more enterprising prospectors, realised that if fortunes were to be made at the gold-field they could be made by freighting rather than digging. After an encounter with a burned-out sourdough prospector (a seasoned gold-miner who made bread from sour dough), who traded his last sled dog for a bag of flour,

Waldren produced the Chinook, a breed of heavy draught dog capable of pulling a heavy 300 lb load; not as quickly as a Siberian husky, but a powerful, useful dog which resembled a spitz-tailed Labrador rather than a conventional husky.

Other southern dogs were interbred with native husky-types to produce strong and speedy sled dogs. London, who spent only a brief while in the gold-fields, was appalled by the adulteration of the native stock and stated that the Athapaskan natives chained their best bitches in the woods to couple with wolves so as to rejuvenate the bloodlines once again. London clearly knew nothing of dogs and precious little of wolves, despite his fascination with the latter. The outland dogs were absorbed by the native huskies and a new type of dog, the Alaskan husky, emerged a faster, stronger, more trainable type than its Siberian husky counterpart.

I ask the reader's forgiveness for the following anecdote concerning the enterprising Treadwell Waldren, who bought up a supply of metal dog bowls at Anchorage and travelled with them to the gold-fields, much to the amusement of fellow dog mushers. In the gold-fields Treadwell Waldren sold these bowls for six hundred times the price he paid for them, for the bowls were ideally suited for the heartbreaking work of panning for gold. The Yukon gold-mining enterprise was a financial disaster – $16,000,000 worth of gold was mined at a cost of $60,000,000! London succeeded in panning only $4.50 worth of gold during an entire winter's work, but journeyed home to San Francisco to become the world's best paid novelist, finally earning an enormous $70,000 in 1917, the year of his death.

The native Alaskan husky, the malamute (a hideous distortion of the word Mahlinuit or Alaskan Eskimo) is a colossal brute and the world's most powerful hauling dog. Its great strength makes it a difficult breed to control by conventional methods. Indeed, the famous Bearpaw Lobo once hauled a double-decker bus along a street as a display of its great strength, and could snap inch-thick sisal ropes at a lunge.

Malamute males are extremely aggressive with other dogs and mushers found it expedient to castrate the males before harnessing them, so as to control their awful aggression, though later in this book I will question the efficiency of castration as a method of controlling aggressive behaviour. Hence the malamute is one of the most unsuitable types of dog for the dog owner to train, yet their great beauty and wild appearance attract hosts of unsuitable owners to buy these aggressive powerhouses.

A slightly different breed from the malamute, the Eskimo dog, is equally difficult to train to accept livestock. The breed, which is often the most attractively coloured spitz-type, has experienced a somewhat mixed response from British dog breeders.

Despite the rigorous selection to which the breed has been subjected over the last ten thousand years or so, the original imported breeding stock carried the genes for epilepsy and 'fitting' puppies were common during the early years of the breed in Britain. Breeders of these gorgeous dogs then took an unprecedented step and refrained from breeding the line but imported epilepsy-free stock from Norway at enormous cost. The breed club members most surely deserve the accolade 'dedicated'.

Why the Fiennes seem prepared to include the German shepherd dog in the classification 'Northern' breeds is a mystery, though Strebel was convinced that the breed-type was originally a spitz-tail type and that breeders had bred out the curly tail which characterises the spitz type. Yet no animal is quite as dissimilar to the sled dogs than the German shepherd dog. No more malleable or docile a type of dog could be found anywhere – indeed, the breed is often awarded the appellation 'the best of dogs', though in the wrong hands it can equally easily degenerate to become the worst of dogs!

It is interesting to note that the continental breeds of herding dog are not only larger but more aggressive than the native British herding dogs such as the Border collie – the wolf is certainly to blame for the dichotomy which exists between the herding types. Continental herding dogs have been bred not only to herd but to defend the flocks against wolves and other large predators. In Britain these large predators became extinct or rare before the herding curs began to refine. Thus breeds such as the Briard, a large, powerful and formidable drover's dog, the Malinois, a duplicate of the early German shepherd dog and many other mastiff-type breeds evolved on the Continent, but Britain tended to favour smaller dogs, of a less aggressive disposition, as herding and droving curs.

Yet the incredible versatility of the German shepherd dog makes it almost unique and quite distinct from the half-wild northern draught dogs to which Fiennes believes the German shepherd dog is related. The supposedly wolf-like shape of the German shepherd dog possibly makes the breed such a suitable and successful guard dog – though no one who has had any contact with wolves would confuse them with German shepherd dogs. Few police forces throughout the world do not employ the services of this breed. For a while the Metropolitan Police Force experimented with the use of Labrador retrievers, powerful and highly intelligent dogs, and the Tokyo Police with Akitas, huge spitz-type dogs with the size, power and appearance of the largest malamutes. At one time the Hong Kong force went through a period when it favoured boxers, Teutonic editions of the British bulldog. Yet each police force finally reverted to the use of German shepherd dogs after experimenting with various other breeds, each of which was found wanting in some respect.

Most security firms, police forces and military establishments use these dogs as guards. They may lack the incredible power of the Rottweiler, the furious speed of a Dobermann and the awesome visage and crushing bite of the bullmastiff, but because of their strange perspicacity they are able to be controlled in an attack situation that would cause another breed to do considerable damage before it could be restrained. A tale will certainly illustrate this point.

A police officer/dog handler was on duty in Manchester when a man approached him in a cordial manner and engaged him in conversation. The man, still smiling and showing no apparent hostility, reached into his coat pocket, suddenly produced a knife and lunged at the police officer. Before he could deliver a killing thrust the German shepherd dog who accompanied the officer had seized the knife arm and pulled the man to the ground, only to find that, despite the intense pain a bite from a German shepherd dog can inflict, the man had switched the knife to the other hand and was attempting to stab the dog. The German shepherd dog promptly seized the other arm and bit so forcefully the assailant was forced to drop the knife. Yet the dog was restrained by a single command when the attacker had dropped the weapon he was holding, and displayed no further hostility to the miscreant on the way to the police station.

Tales of the strange perspicacity these dogs possess are legion. Lucas, author of *Hunt and Working Terriers*, had a curious respect for the intelligence of the breed. Lucas was captured by the Germans during World War I and because his toes had become gangrenous he was given some freedom, for he was expected to die. Lucas was made of sterner stuff, however, and amputated his toes and affected an escape. Two of his fellow prisoners apparently 'borrowed' German uniforms and also attempted to leave the camp. However two German shepherd dogs instantly identified the two prisoners, despite the fact they had been overlooked by other guards. Lucas always refrained from telling the fate of the two would-be escapees, but one could guess at the outcome of the tale!

The German shepherd dog has a formidable record as a search and rescue dog – a role once credited only to that alpine mastiff, the St Bernard. For some inexplicable reason, herding dogs have keen olfactory senses, though it is difficult to explain why, as a sheep dog or cattle dog needs little by way of sense of smell to perform the tasks for which it was bred. The sense of smell is strongly developed in the German shepherd dog and is of great use to those who use their dogs to track down people who have been buried under snow drifts. Some German shepherd dogs have incredible records of finds, particularly dogs bred on the Continent where there are awards for dogs which qualify as tracker dogs – a practice now being copied by British dog handlers. Yet there are those, who are not *au fait* with mountain rescue, who believe that the German shepherd dog is not the ideal search and rescue dog because of its frame and disposition. It is argued that a person who has been buried under snow for some time could be in a state of deep shock. Hence the appearance of

The German shepherd dog

A white German shepherd dog

a type of dog that is well known for its 'attack' qualities may well exacerbate the condition of the victim. Apparently the ideal type of dog for such a role would be a family pet type dog, such as a spaniel or collie, which would not inspire fear in the trapped victim. Yet the German shepherd dog is still the most popular search and rescue dog in the Alps where many climbers fall victim to the vagaries of inclement weather.

If the German shepherd dog is one of the most versatile dogs, the title must also be shared by the Border collie – that most uniquely British breed of herding dog which, because of its incredible perspicacity and adaptability, has supplanted other herding breed throughout the world. Shepherds in Patagonia use the breed, as do Australian sheep farmers, despite the fact that there are many native breeds of sheep and cattle dogs in Australasia. No dog seems more at home herding sheep on the rough terrain of Mexico, where the dog must not only cope with rock screes and ravines, but endure extremes of temperature and a low protein diet, but then this might be expected of a dog which the Fiennes consider to be a relatively pure descendant of the northern wolf.

It must seem very strange that a creature that is as antipathetic to sheep as the northern Palaearctic wolf should have been domesticated to provide animals suitable for herding the same sheep, yet there are marked similarities between hunting and herding – in fact only the element of restraint creates a dichotomy between the two qualities. I ask the reader to observe the almost unwholesome fervour with which the collie creeps towards its sheep, and the excited way it drives the flock towards the shepherd (coupled with the reluctance of most collies to drive the sheep away from the dog handler). Herding is in fact simply a sublimated form of hunting where the shepherd emulates the role of the pack alpha male. The sheep are driven towards this alpha male which sets about and slays the prey. Hunting involves the killing of prey; herding is the blow stopping short, so to speak. Indeed, once collies unleash this latent desire to slay sheep they become the very worst of stock worriers. The restrained hunting qualities manifested by collies are utilised by breeders of lurchers, who use greyhounds to give the lurcher speed but blend this speed with the furtive hunting instinct manifested by collies – and of course, the incredible intelligence for which the collie is famed.

Prior to the coming of the railway system, which allowed the British to explore these islands more easily and quickly, each district produced a type of collie. From Essex to Norfolk, blue and brown bearded type collies were popular. In Snowdon a lean, mean, untidy looking blue collie, courageous enough to face down half-wild goats, was favoured. In Cumberland a more robust prick-eared collie, similar to some of the sheep dogs found in the Cevennes, was prized, while north of Inverness the bearded collie was popular with shepherds who grazed the Cheviot sheep (the Great Sheep of the post clearance days), and with those who rejected the new ways imposed by the Duke of Sutherland and still kept the half-wild Highland cattle instead of sheep. Drovers still moved mixed flocks of sheep, goats, cattle and geese with leggy, often emaciated looking dogs known collectively as Smithfield collies – dogs famed for their incredible homing instinct. One was regularly sold 'to Englishmen' at Falkirk market but once released by its new owners would head north and swim from Kyle to Skye. It is believed that the epic tale *Lassie Come Home* was inspired by the deeds of this rough-coated droving dog, which was a star's flight from the dolichocephalic rough collies seen in the 'Lassie' films.

However, once the railways allowed shepherds to explore other areas of Britain the tocsin was sounded for the various breeds of herding dog. On the Borders between Scotland and England a distinctive type of sheep dog had developed, a lightly-built, quicksilver type of dog that was apparently every shepherd's dream. This herding dog was a creeping collie quite distinct from the collies which walked their sheep towards the shepherd, and accompanying this creeping quality was a tractability that made the dog a pleasure to own. In less than thirty years the Border had either absorbed or replaced most of the native breeds of collie, which in many ways was a pity, for the other strains of collie had much to commend them. Dr Phillpotts, a regular contributor to the magazine *The Ark*, a booklet which caters for the interests of those concerned with endangered breeds of livestock, laments the passing of the bob-tailed Irish collie, a breed which, while it was an efficient herder, would desist from rounding up sheep when it was not required to do so. These bush collies, at least according to Phillpotts, could exist on a frugal diet that would starve a Border collie, and there were other breeds possessing unique and useful qualities that might pass into extinction when the Border collie became popular.

Yet the versatility of this breed of dog is little short of phenomenal and there seems little the breed cannot be taught to do. Reports of collies working as gun dogs are legion, and their reputation for being gentle dogs (not always justified, one must add) has endeared them to search and rescue dog trainers, for reasons already explained. They are usually a little too quicksilver to be suitable as guide dogs for the blind, though some have been successfully trained for this role, but as drug-seeking dogs the breed must be considered as good as some of the best strains of springer spaniel.

During the early days of obedience tests German shepherd dogs and spaniels competed successfully against all other breeds, but their success was to be short-lived. Within ten years of the inception of obedience trials, strains of Border collie had begun to appear which, while they sometimes lacked a little in herding instinct, were tailored to compete and win at these obedience trials. They worked closely with their handlers, displayed an almost mechanical obedience to command and had pronounced scent-determining qualities. The days of other breeds of dogs winning at the topmost level at these trials had come to an end. Most obedience champions today are Border collies.

The breed seems almost purpose bred for the now very popular agility tests which involve the dog running over and under a series of obstacles – against the clock, so to speak. Border collies are more agile than German shepherd dogs, more biddable than spaniels and faster than any of the toy breeds which won well at the earlier agility tests. Furthermore, the Border collie matures quickly and can be used for competition work at an age when the German shepherd dog is still very infantile.

David Ashpool, the Caithnessian dog handler and guard dog trainer, is of the opinion that 'other breeds' tests which deliberately exclude Border collies from competing will need to be devised – a recent change in the rules for protection dog tests allow a dog to qualify if it barks at or menaces (as if attacking a 'criminal'), have placed Border collies in the forefront as competition dogs in yet another test.

Ashpool is of the opinion that it is only a matter of time before some breeders of Border collies decide to produce a larger, heavier, stronger type of collie that may well replace the German shepherd dog as the universal police dog. It is true that few Border collies have the menacing visage of a black-muzzled German shepherd dog but cosmetic qualities can so easily be bred into a strain. Once this new type of Border collie has been developed it will be only a matter of a short period of time before the Border collie becomes the most flexible and suitable police dog, and yet another domain will have been conquered by this the most versatile of the northern group of working dogs.

Yet the Border collie is not the only collie to be worked in Britain. In some districts the bearded collie is still worked, though readers who are accustomed to the sight of exhibition bearded collies would not recognise the working strains as being of the same breed. There are many theories as to the origin of this hardy and intelligent dog. Mrs Willison, who was the forerunner in the formation of the Bearded Collie Club, believes that the breed arrived in Britain in the sixteenth century when a Gdansk ship arrived in Scotland to transport black-faced sheep to Poland. Local dogs failed to drive the black-faced sheep, which are notoriously wild, up the gangplank of the bobbing and rolling ship so the captain of the ship, one Kasirmirez, produced two sheep dogs which set about the black-faced sheep with a vengeance and drove them into the holds. So impressed were the local shepherds that they traded two fine horned rams for the dogs and hence the bearded collie arrived in Britain. There may be some substance to this tale, for the Polish Lowland sheep dog bears a strong resemblance to the bearded collie, but there is a more likely explanation for the origin of the beardie. It is likely that either Celtic or Germanic tribes brought the type out of eastern Europe during their migrations, as the type is found as far south as the Spanish Meseta and as far north as Norway.

Bearded collies also fell out of popularity before the conquering march of the Border collie. Bearded collies are usually more game and surly than their Border counterparts. Indeed, many have courage enough to turn enraged bulls, or face down hostile black-faced rams, the breed of sheep for which bearded collies were bred to herd and drive. Broader in the head than most Border collies, the beardie may well have a trace of mastiff in its make-up, though Logan, one of the authorities on the breed type, relates that at one time shepherds were known to introduce a dash of deerhound blood to give the beardie extra leg length to cope with the terrain over which these dogs were intended to work. That some form of sight hound blood – greyhound or deerhound – entered into the make-up of certain collies is widely believed. Many authorities believe that the Smithfield collie, a strain that has yet to be adequately described, was in fact a combination of some type of herding dog with a strong dash of greyhound – as much a lurcher as a true collie, in fact.

Bearded collies fell out of favour for many reasons. Some strains have a marked aversion to the lead, but all strains are slower to mature than conventional Border collies and lack the Border's characteristic 'style' while herding. Some strains of creeping bearded collie once existed, beardies that worked sheep in much the same manner as the Border collie. Indeed, the famous Grampian breeder, A.H.W. Grant, who died in 1991, kept a strain that was known locally as the Dallas red (Dallas being a town in the Grampians), but this strain also became rare after the death of Grant.

Beardies have hirsute coats which tend to ball-up in winter – the coat becomes a knotted tangle of plant material, mud and sometimes snow – and, while this jacket may give the breed some protection from the ferocity of a Highland winter, it never-the-less gives the dog a messy and unkempt appearance. Tom Muirhead, who retired from his post as a hill shepherd in 1992 and is considered by many as the last great authority on the working bearded collie, states that in the early part of the century the shepherds of Skye (and many of the best modern strains of working bearded collie originated on that island), were wont to shear the dogs as well as the sheep at shearing time, and weighed the dog hair together with the coarse stapled black-faced sheep fleeces. It was generally believed that with the passing of A.H.W. Grant and the premature retirement of Muirhead the working bearded collie is doomed to extinction. However, this does not appear to be the case. Two quite distressing eye abnormalities have appeared in the best working Border collie strains – collie eye anomaly and the more distressing progressive retinal atrophy, a disease that only manifests itself during the dog's second year. These defects are not inherent amongst working bearded collies. Likewise, in the last few years certain otherwise good working strains of Border collie have started to produce dogs which are ill at ease with hostile sheep. Turnbull, who owned the famous bearded collie Blue, once advertised his beardie at stud to Border collie bitches which were a shade short on courage, for Blue (one of the only beardies to have secured a position on the sheep dog register) was a fearless dog who sired equally game offspring.

In recent years lurcher breeders have tended to use bearded collies or bearded/Border composites to produce good running dogs. Bearded collie blood tends to confer courage to the progeny, good strong feet for which the 'rock and heather' herding beardie is famous, and a thick, tear resistant hide. At the National Lurcher and Racing Club trials at Blairgowrie in 1992 the entire Scottish entry was beardie/Border bred.

The rough collie, the type of collie popularly known as the Lassie type is something of an enigma. The breed type was clearly related to the Border collie but exhibition breeders have certainly brought in borzoi blood, or the blood of some other greyhound type, to improve the coat and give the breed the dolichocephalic head-type which is certainly not typical of the British herding dog. The rough collie and its miniaturised form, the Shetland sheep dog, is seldom worked and possesses few of the qualities manifested by its sheep herding ancestors. The glabrous form of the breed type, referred to as the smooth collie, does in fact closely resemble a lurcher in shape and head structure.

If the Fiennes are correct in including the terriers of Britain under the heading 'The Northern Group', then that vast family the scent hounds, that hunt by scent rather than sight, must also be included in this group, for terriers are probably hounds bred down in size and given a dash of bulldog blood to improve their courage. However, while Fiennes and Dunbar include the terrier in their Northern Group classification, the scent hounds are classified under the heading Mastiff Group which would therefore place the terrier under this group as well, as, according to Fiennes and Dunbar, both the scent hounds and the bulldog belong to the mastiff group.

However, as it is expedient to follow the classification advocated by the Fiennes, we shall include the terriers under the classification Northern Group no matter how inaccurate this heading may be. Terriers are uniquely British. No other country seems to have developed anything akin to the terrier, though the Germans developed a small hound called the dachshund to seek out and help catch badgers, foxes and rabbits. Why the British were unique in wishing to develop any breed of animal akin to the terrier has long been debated by cynologists. Perhaps the early extinction of larger predators such as the wolf, the bear, and to a certain extent the boar encouraged the sporting Briton to develop breeds of dog suitable for seeking out and destroying smaller predators such as the otter, the fox and the badger.

It is highly likely that the very first terriers were simply small hounds. Indeed Jaques de Foilleux in 1560 refers to the dogs he uses to dig badgers as bassets and many early types of terrier sported the splayed feet

The terrier – a uniquely British breed of dog

that characterise the basset hound of today – the 'Queen Anne' legs of many pre-1960 Jack Russells would in fact suggest that a basset or similar hound featured strongly in their ancestry.

Whatever the ancestry of the terrier – and it is most certainly bred from hounds of some sort – by the eighteenth century a distinctive terrier type seems to have emerged; a type referred to as the Old English rough coated black and tan terrier – a rather misleading title, for these terriers were sometimes blue and tan, black and tan, tan black grizzled or brindled. Likewise the jackets sported by these dogs were rough, broken or smooth – though positive information on the breed is hard to come by. It is likely that while the type, as a true breed, perhaps became extinct in the late nineteenth century, it persisted as the fell terrier and the primitive Welsh terriers such as were bred at Ynysfor since 1760. Horner, in *Terriers of the World*, refers to this terrier as the Old Adam of terriers.

These terriers were used to flush otters and foxes from their holes and earths, or by baying fix the badger below ground so that those so inclined might dig to it and capture the animal. At this time badgers found a ready market. Taplin, a gynaecological surgeon, deplored the action of badger baiting and applauded the action of the magistrates of Islington and Tottenham Court Road, London, who sought to put an end to the activity which 'brought together an infinity of the most abandoned miscreants with their terriers and bull dogs from every extremity of the town'. However, diggers at the time when Taplin wrote his oft-quoted *Sportsman's Cabinet* (1803) found the sport of badger digging a very lucrative one. The beast could be sold to baiters for as much as a guinea, for the badger is a formidable opponent and 'will endure a great deal of brutal treatment before it gives up the ghost and dies'. Dead 'their fat is in high estimation with rustics for ointments and salves', while the skin was used 'for hard-wearing fusile rugs, holsters for pistols and sporrans for Highlanders'.

Yet much as Taplin despised the sport of badger baiting (quite distinct from badger digging, for baiting became illegal in 1835 while the action of digging badgers became an offence only in 1973) he had nothing but admiration for terriers and found them to be the 'most useful and pleasurable of dogs'.

He praises the courage of these diminutive dogs and relates a tale of how a young gentleman called Hardie, accompanied by his terrier, was passing through St Andrew's Square, Glasgow, when he was beset by a footpad armed with a club. The dog promptly flew at the footpad and seized him by the throat, enabling Hardie to snatch the club and run for safety. His terrier found its way home later carrying with it half the man's waistcoat into which was sown a guinea piece.

Sir Walter Scott also praises the terrier as a guard dog and relates a curious tale to illustrate the worth of the terrier. Scott, a barrister by trade, successfully defended a burglar who was obviously guilty and Scott was given a piece of advice by the miscreant, who suggested that Scott should always keep a small terrier dog which would be permanently awake and give tongue when a burglar entered the house, rather than a mastiff-sized dog which would often be asleep. Scott was in fact instrumental in the naming of a breed of terrier, the Dandie Dinmont, which was named after a sporting squire who appears in the pages of Scott's disjointed and badly conceived book *Guy Mannering*. Scott never met James Davidson of Hindlee, supposedly the breeder of the prototype Dandie Dinmont, but Davidson made large sums of money selling his terriers after Scott popularised the breed type. To unravel the pedigrees of Davidson's dogs has proved impossible for he called all his terriers either Pepper or Mustard.

Yet changes were afoot to alter the shape and disposition of the terrier. The sport of badger baiting, arguably the most unpleasant sport devised by man (though this title is shortly to be contested, I'm afraid), became popular and to perpetuate this atrocity a new type of terrier began to appear. To create this new type of terrier, breeders mated the native black and tan terriers to that devil incarnate, that fiend in canine form, the English bulldog, of which more will be told later. As many of the best strains of pit bulldog were white, small white terriers began to appear, one of which Taplin persuaded the artist Reinagle to paint, and which produced puppies which Taplin sold for £3 a piece in 1800 – a huge sum to pay for a terrier at that time. From this union of black and tan terrier and bulldog came the smooth fox terrier and the sundry Jack Russell types (and perhaps the Sealyham terrier), though Casle, in *Monograph of the Fox Terrier*, believes that the fox terrier is of great antiquity and may simply be a white sport of the old English black and tan terrier.

Yet another sport was to produce a change in the working terriers of the time, namely what was referred to as ratting, though to associate this practice with legitimate rat-hunting is indeed an insult to hunting. A dozen or so rats were tipped into an enclosure and a dog placed on the floor of the pit and encouraged to slay the rats. The dog which killed the greatest number of rats in the shortest period of time was deemed the winner of the event. Rats bite hard and cause a dog considerable pain in doing so. Hence dogs taking part in the above activity needed to be fast, hard biting and pain resistant and so yet more bulldog blood was added to the native terrier stock. It is highly likely that both the Staffordshire bull terrier and the miniature bull terrier were created from the cross-breeding. Tiny dogs were greatly prized in the rat pits and the sight of a small, fragile terrier killing large sewer rats attracted huge crowds, including the Duke of Wellington, and famous dogs such as the miniature black and tan terrier Tiny were as famous as Shakespeare's bears Sackerson and Old Hulks. Very small bull terriers were often tremendous ratters. Pony Queen, a tiny brute of under three pounds in weight, was bred by Sir Raymond Tyrriot Wilson in 1906. Larger hybrids, faster and harder biting, whose speed was increased by a dash of greyhound blood, would later become known as Manchester terriers and perhaps even whippets owe their origins to these crossbreeds.

It is highly likely that the Irish terriers, the Kerry Blue, the Irish terrier, the Glen of Imaal and the soft-coated Wheaten terriers, share a common origin, but are fairly pure forms of the old English terrier little adulterated with bulldog blood or with further addition of hound blood that was added to give bulldog-blooded terriers voice to direct the digger to the spot where the terrier kept its quarry at bay. Irish terriers are usually mute and are reluctant to give tongue at their foes, preferring to engage and fight the quarry.

The origin of the Scottish breeds of terrier is confused though the type is certainly antique. John Caius in his letters to Conrad Gesner (c.1570) mentions them and it appears as though the Cairn, the Skye,

The Airedale

the Scottish or Aberdeen terrier have changed remarkably little since that time. In character they are quite distinct from their English and Welsh counterparts though they were bred to perform the same tasks. Most English and Welsh terriers pack fairly readily, possibly due to their hound ancestry. Scottish breeds refuse to pack and often ten terriers will hunt ten separate lines when hunting.

However, before leaving the subject of terriers, it is perhaps expedient to mention that giant terrier, the Airedale, an enlarged replica of the Lakeland and the Welsh terrier, perhaps, but so big that it is virtually impossible for this terrier to go to ground. Why anyone would wish to create a terrier-shaped animal that measures as much as 24 inches at the shoulder is a mystery. Tale has it that ratters working the banks of the river Aire in Yorkshire wanted a large terrier with an affinity for water. Terriers catching rats swimming in deep water are unable to kill their catches until their feet touch solid ground and hence often receive terrible damage from their rats. Hence a tall terrier which might be able to stand in deep water and kill its rats was perhaps desirable. Personally I believe such tales are rubbish and that the North Yorkshire terrier fancier, or perhaps artisan hunter would best describe this type of sportsman, simply wanted a large utility-type dog that would catch rats, rabbits, perhaps otters and even act as a guard dog. Dog fighting was rife around the Aire and hence spirited terriers were considered desirable for a while. Dog fighting is an ugly activity but it ensured that only courageous dogs were used to create the Airedale terrier.

The origin of this huge terrier is a mystery. It has been suggested that the breed was simply an overgrown form of that Old Adam of terriers the old English rough-coated black and tan terrier, but the early specimens had a decidedly houndy look about them. In fact C.H. Lane in *All About Dogs* (1900) suggests that the appellation terrier should not be applied to the Airedale, which should really be categorised as a hound.

Colonel David Hancock in *The Heritage of the Dog* shares the same opinion as Lane and believes that the Airedale was a fairly pure form of the rough-coated Lancashire hounds that were used to hunt a variety of quarry in the north of England. These hounds, similar to the old Welsh harrier, were not only wonderful hunters but were aggressive and quarrelsome and closely resembled early prints of untrimmed Airedales.

Lucas, in *Hunt and Working Terriers* (1931), is a little more pedantic about the origin of these great terriers and suggests that when Barney Ottershaw (a singularly appropriate name) was Master of Otterhounds, a local character obtained an illicit mating from the hound Thunder to a bull terrier bitch and the Airedale is descended from this union. Later Irish terrier blood was certainly used to refine the dog, but even the origin of this type and the modern Airedale is a far cry from its houndy unattractive ancestor.

It is impossible to mention the Airedale without mentioning the incredible versatility of the breed. Before the Plott hound became popular in America, big game hunters regularly used Airedale lines to hunt bear, puma, ocelot, jaguar and razor-back wild boar. The breed had its limitations as a big game hunter, however, for its high courage, conferred by its bull and Irish terrier ancestors perhaps, encouraged it to tackle game rather than bringing it to bay and hence the life-expectancy of these terriers was short. Ben Lilly, who accompanied Roosevelt on his immortal Teddy Bear hunt, stated that he refrained from using Airedales simply because they tended to fight bears rather than bay at them.

Yet the Airedale must certainly be considered the most versatile of terriers. During the 1914–1918 war, a war that alerted the world to the amazing capabilities of the German shepherd dog, British military dog trainers used Airedales for the same purposes as the Germans used the German shepherd dog. Colonel Richardson, one of the most famous of the military dog trainers, considered the Airedale to be if anything a better guard dog than the German shepherd dog, having the terrier's alert nature and the strength to follow and confront an intruder. In his advertisement in 1925 he states of Airedales 'The best watch dog . . . suitable guards for ladies living alone', but unlike most terriers 'not quarrelsome'. In the previous year, Richardson had penned his book *Watch Dogs*, a book that is simply a eulogy on the virtues extant in this breed.

More outlandish still is the advertisement of one Metcalf, in Lucas' *Pedigree Dog Breeding*, who offers dogs 'over distemper', an important consideration prior to the perfection of vaccines, and specially trained so that ladies may handle them (so many advertisements offered dogs as guards for ladies during this time that one must consider it is likely that women living on their own must have been very vulnerable in the 1920s), and able to detect and drive away tramps. Some of his dogs were 'holy terrors' that 'will face bricks and sticks' yet continue to guard. Metcalf's advertisement is now considered as a collector's piece by the dog world today.

As a group terriers are usually fairly quarrelsome, though certain breeds such as Borders and Welsh terriers are somewhat slower to fight, and, because their natural duties require them to bark at their quarry, most are prone to be noisy. Their ebullient nature demands that these dogs are exercised regularly and the majority are still enthusiastic hunters, despite the fact that few are purposely bred to hunt these days. Terriers will usually run to ground after rabbits and foxes so it is seldom safe to allow even the most blue-blooded exhibition animal a chance to run free where fox or badger settes are numerous. Ralph Hodgson, the one-man rescue service from Newcastle on Tyne, was called out many times to rescue hunt terriers that had run to ground, but his most regular customers were two West Highland white terriers that ran to ground at the first opportunity. Both had been sired by Crufts winners but followed any fox or badger to ground. Eventually both disappeared without trace so one must surmise their fate.

Amazingly Fiennes places the Chihuahua in the Northern Group though the breed bears little resemblance to the great grey northern wolf. The origin of this curious and enchanting toy breed is obscure. Dunbar, in *Dog Behaviour*, suggests that the breed is descended from the Techichi, a heavily-boned, long-haired breed kept by the Toltec Indians in the ninth century. Dunbar also suggests that when the Toltecs were overrun by the Aztec in the sixteenth century the Aztec crossed the Techichi with the hairless dog and produced the Chihuahua. Yet neither Bernal Diaz De Castillo, who accompanied Cortez in his expedition against the Aztecs, nor Prescott in the *History of Mexico*, make mention of the breeding of this diminutive dog.

The Mastiff Group

The Fiennes consider that the mastiff is a descendant of the large and fierce Tibetan wolf, *Canis lupus chaneo* or *laniger*, a broad-headed, strong jawed wolf. However, there is some evidence to suggest that all these head types, brachycephalic (broad-headed), mesocephalic (medium broad-headed), and dolichocephalic (narrow-headed), appear in the same litter born to European wolves.

Typical mastiff-types are broad-headed, strong jawed, short faced with particularly punishing masseter muscles operating their jaws. Dunbar suggests that the type originated in the mountain chain that stretches from the Pyrenees to Tibet. There is some evidence to dispute Dunbar's claim that the breed was originally developed to guard flocks for there is proof that both the Assyrians and Egyptians ran 'bobbery packs' of mixed dog breeds, the faster ones being required to run the prey beast down and the more powerful ones being used to seize, hold or kill the quarry. It seems likely that shepherds simply used strong powerful dogs to guard the flocks and the breed type was not specifically developed for herding work.

The long-coated Tibetan mastiff has seldom been seen in Britain and few would recognise this huge and ferocious dog. The Tibetan dog used by Graham in the creation of the Irish wolfhound breeding programme was in all probability simply a large powerful dog of mixed origin whose owner applied the appellation 'Tibetan' in order to sell the beast, or to suggest it had exotic origins. During the fifteenth century any exotic-looking animal sported the title Turkish! Yet the Tibetan mastiff certainly does exist and is the most feared of guards. Briin, writing of the curious tribe the Black Lola, which practises polyandry, possibly because of the high mortality rate of the women during childbirth, suggests that the tribe practises two methods of birth control: the oldest uncles become monks and practise celibacy and someone has to feed the mastiffs! These dogs were kept by herdsmen and householders alike and were dangerous to both intruders and wild beasts.

What Alexander the Great encountered during his trip to Bactria was almost certainly a mastiff-type which set about tigers and Indian lions with great fury. His accounts of these fights were probably conveyed to his tutor, Aristotle, who concluded, quite wrongly, that the striped brindle (tiger bridle) colouring of these mastiffs indicated that these dogs were bred by chaining bitches in the forest to await the amorous advances of tigers. Oppian simply plagiarized Aristotle's notions.

Yet the Greeks certainly knew of the mastiff-type dogs long before Alexander's conquests in Asia. Herodotus mentions that these dogs were the constant companions of Hyrcannian and Molossian hunter/herdsmen from northern Greece to the shores of the Caspian Sea and these heavy-jawed dogs were certainly able to kill wolves that attacked flocks and herds. The terrible bite that can be inflicted by a mastiff defies belief and this, coupled with the strong hunting instinct still present in the breed, makes a mastiff of any sort an awesome adversary.

Whether or not the mastiff or a mastiff-type was brought to Britain by the Phoenicians or by the migrating Celts from central Europe is debatable, though one should have serious doubts about the influence the Phoenicians had on these islands. If J.G. Millais is correct in his assumptions that these Semitic travellers introduced the variety of animals he claimed they did, then galleys must have resembled floating arks rather than trading vessels. The Celts certainly would have had contact with mastiff types and brought them with them when they migrated from central Europe and southern Russia.

Whatever the origin of the British mastiff, this country was destined to become famous for its ferocious dogs. The mastiff-type was of little use in the pursuit of deer for its huge, cumbersome shape prevented it from coming to terms with these creatures, but it was brave enough, or perhaps foolhardy enough, to face a boar, the only creature which will stand and fight long before it is brought to bay. Shakespeare had little knowledge of this creature for by Elizabethan times the boar had become so rare that the aristocracy kept the beasts in walled enclosures, feeding them on household waste and the lees of fermented beer, but he wrote of the beast 'and when he strikes his crooked tushes slay' (Venus and Adonis). To face such an animal a dog must be either inordinately brave or remarkably foolish and, in all probability, the mastiff was regarded as a suicidal maniac by those who kept them. Again Shakespeare, in *Henry V*, relates the dialogue between two French nobles prior to the Battle of Agincourt:

> Rambures: 'That Island of England breeds very valiant creatures; their mastiffs are of unmatchable courage.'
>
> Orleans: 'Foolish curs that run winking into the mouth of a Russian bear and have their heads crushed like rotten apples.'

The Celts also used these dogs in battle as Caesar's Gallic Wars attests and these mastiffs were almost certainly bred in Britain. After the invasion of these islands the market for trained fighting dogs made it profitable for *bestiarii* to breed and train these animals for combat in the arenas. Quintus Arius Symmachus records that these dogs were often so ferocious that they needed to be brought to Rome in iron cages and

Martial describes the concern these animals caused in the arena. Their awesome courage and their terrible biting power made them incredibly dangerous opponents.

On the field of battle these mastiffs caused confusion amongst the enemy, attacking both the enemy and their horses. Their bites paralysed limbs or tore pieces from their opponents. They unhorsed riders by seizing the throats of their steeds and were foes to be feared, but it was the confusion the mastiff attacks caused that made an army using these dogs a terrible foe. When hurt or wounded these mastiffs retaliated furiously and the very presence of such dogs inspired dread, but it was not long before the Roman soldiery in Gaul learned to deal with these beasts in the field of combat.

Later the mastiff was to become the insignia of British courage, tenacity and fidelity. It would be used as a guard dog and a perspicacious guard at that. If I might leap forward in time just a little to illustrate a point, Sir Henry Lee of Ditchley kept a chained mastiff in his yard – most mastiffs spent their days on the end of chains and were often referred to as banded (chained) dogs, later to be corrupted to 'ban' dogs. The dog lived a miserable life, perhaps, but one day escaped the chain and crawled into Sir Henry's bedroom. At midnight an Italian valet crept in quietly and was attacked by the furious mastiff, whereupon the terrified valet confessed he had been sent to murder Lee as he slept.

However, even the mastiff, seemingly immutable since prehistory, was about to undergo changes in its shape and structure. In 1209 some weeks before Christmas, William, Earl Warrenne, was attracted by the sight of two aged bulls fighting and the herdsmen, seeking to break the battle perhaps, urging furious ban dogs (often used to drive aggressive cattle) on to the antagonists. The sight so intrigued the Earl that he decided that some six weeks before Christmas an elderly bull should be secured and battered to death before the crowds assembled to watch the carnage. The meat from this horribly mutilated beast would then be butchered and given to the poor of the town of Stamford.

The sport, if such an outrage should be afforded such an appellation, became incredibly popular and would later include baits involving bears, boars and elderly crotchety horses, and it seems almost inevitable that dogs would be deliberately bred to perform at such events. The huge and often ungainly mastiff was obviously too cumbersome to avoid the horns of the bull, the claws of the bear or the cutting, slashing tushes of the boar, so smaller mastiffs, faster dogs, began to be bred, dogs which still possessed the awesome bite of the mastiff but were more agile and less likely to be hurt if hurled into the air by a bull or bear. It is worth mentioning that these small, degenerate mastiffs were so prized by their owners that various ne'er-do-wells were paid to watch the bait and as soon as a dog was cast by the horns of the bull to rush forward and allow their own backs to break the dog's fall.

These degenerate mastiffs would later be referred to as bulldogs but it was not until 1631 that reference to this new breed appeared in print. In a letter from Prestwick Eaton, residing in Spain as a merchant's agent, to a friend in London he requests, 'procure me two good bull dogs and let them be sent by the first ship. Let them be good at the bull and cost what they will'. Such was the value an Englishman placed on his bull dog.

The great passion the English displayed for mastiffs and bulldogs was to inspire the first dog encyclopedia, *The British Dog* (1576), penned by John Keyes, who wrote under the pseudonym of John Caius – a latinised form of Keyes. Keyes struck up a relationship with one Conrad Gesner, a Swiss naturalist who was fascinated with the English love of the mastiff. Hence he wrote to Keyes to enquire about mastiffs and British dogs in general. Why Gesner singled out Keyes is a mystery, for despite the latter's reputation for being both an academic and a prolific author, Keyes had not the slightest interest in dogs. Keyes, however, systematically categorised dogs and under the heading Country Dogs he refers to the mastiff.

Clearly the Continentals were intrigued by the Englishmen's love – if love indeed is the correct word – of a good mastiff, and ambassadors to the English court were invariably treated to a day's entertainment at a bear or bull bait. Queen Elizabeth, who was never known to attend a play, was an ardent fan of the bear and bull bait and stated that it was better for the crowd to satiate its blood-lust by attending a bait than spending its time forming idle and disorderly bands in the street. The Priory Council did in fact order that theatres should be closed on Thursdays lest they attract the crowds away from the bull and bear baits.

Shakespeare too attended these baits regularly and mentions famous bears such as Sackerson and Harry Hunks, two bears which survived scores of baits and maimed and killed dozens of mastiffs. Shakespeare refers to Sackerson, who was prone to break his chain and run amok in the audience, in *The Merry Wives of Windsor* when he credits Abraham Slender with the impossible feat of having taken Sackerson by the chain some twenty times when the beast broke its tether. Sordid and grisly as these baits would have been and costly too, for bears would need to be imported from Russia, we are still reminded of these spectacles at Kennel Club shows when rosettes are awarded to the winners of various classes. Rosettes or strips of ribbon were affixed with tar to the hides of bulls and bears about to be baited. The more headstrong or ferocious bulldog and mastiff would often break off a particularly savage attack with a rosette or ribbon attached to its fur, a harmless, innocent reminder of one of the most brutal sports Britain has ever devised.

However popular baiting sports and the breeding of half-mad mastiffs was in Elizabethan England, the activities experienced even greater royal patronage during the reign of James I, who, despite his apparent erudition, relished a feast of gore. So great was the indignation aroused amongst the Puritans, an increasingly popular sect, at the King's fondness for this sport, that James was persuaded to prohibit baiting on Sundays, though the practice was a shade too popular to ban on the other days of the week.

James had long cherished a desire to see how English mastiffs would fare against a lion – an incongruous and predictable contest, one must add – and having discovered that lions were kept in a menagerie in the Tower of London, he encouraged that curious character Edward Alleyn to purchase three game mastiffs at the Paris Gardens. Alleyn, who not only sent hundreds of mastiffs growling to their deaths in the bull and bear pit, but was also a famous philanthropist, procured the mastiffs and the carnage began. The first two mastiffs to be set at the lion died most horribly, but the third attacked the lion with such fury that the beast retreated to its den. James, who firmly believed in the Divine Right of Kings ('Kings are by God appointed and damned are they who do resist or touch the Lord's anointed'), promptly charged Alleyn never to fight this mastiff again for the great dog had bested the King of Beasts and should never again be expected to prove its mettle against a lesser creature.

Alleyn enjoyed the role of ' "Chief Master" ruler and overseer of all and singular games of bears and bulls and mastiff dogs and bitches' – a rather unpopular post for, so great was the King's interest in baiting that Alleyn had the right and power to seize any dogs be considered suitable for training for the pits. Some of the collectors of these dogs were savagely abused and injured by owners of beloved mastiffs who were reluctant to see their pets carried away for training for the ring. Other towns agreed to send dogs to Alleyn but begged not to be sent the 'odious collectors'. Manchester, quite a small town at the time, agreed to provide one fine mastiff dog and a fine mastiff bitch for the bear garden each year.

Charles I like his father James adored the bear gardens, but Cromwell abhorred baiting and had a particular dislike of mastiffs. It is said that this dislike was due at least in part to the fact that as a student he had been set upon by a mastiff, or according to one of Cromwell's biographers, Goldwin Smith, two mastiffs attacked the youth and drove him back against a tree. Here Cromwell attempted to perform what is always regarded as an old wives' tale method of defeating or terrifying a mastiff – namely throwing one's head at the beast. Sampson states that the youth seized his head in his hands and pretended to hurl his head at the dogs. Apparently the gesture worked, for Cromwell lived to tell his tale, and an attack from two mastiffs would most certainly kill a grown man. Shakespeare in *King Lear* mentions the trick: 'Edgar, "Tom will throw his head at them, Avaunt you curs".'

Cromwell did in fact send the extremely thorough and pious zealot,

The bullmastiff

Colonel Pride, to bring an end to the bear pits and cock pits, Pride personally shooting all the bears and wringing the necks of the game cocks. The incredible interest in the ferocious carnage that took place in the pits came to an end, for neither Charles II or James II showed the slightest interest in the blood baths which had so entertained their ancestors.

Yet the degenerate or small mastiffs, short-nosed mastiffs or bulldogs continued to be bred and baited at bulls and somewhat infrequently at bears, for bears were incredibly costly to import from Russia. The bull bait was still regarded as a popular activity some six weeks before Christmas when a live bull was decked and adorned before being turned loose in the streets of Stamford and Tutbury. 'Come all you bonny baiting boys who love to bait the bonny bull'. However in 1802 a Quaker, Pease, persuaded Parliament to pass a bill to outlaw baiting and Parliament complied, somehow avoiding inference to bull baiting which continued until 1835 when it became illegal. In defiance Stamford held out against the edict and staged the bait until 1837, when a troupe of cavalry was despatched to end the bait and the bill for this exercise sent to the mayor. Tale has it some parts of Lancashire continued to allow the baiting of bulls until 1840 but thereafter the outrage seems to have ceased.

The British are by their very nature the most perverse of races for no sooner had bull baiting fallen out of favour than there was an upsurge in the sport of dog fighting. It seems likely that if the 1835 act had not been passed, dog fighting and bull baiting would have slithered into extinction. The baits were attended by whores, pimps, cut-purses and robbers and hence the god-fearing people of the district avoided such activities, but the abolition of baiting gave new life to the illegal sport of dog fighting and produced further changes in the degenerate mastiff type known at that time as the bulldog. The furious, awful bite of the bulldog obviously made the beast an ideal fighting dog – indeed, the dog's incredible resistance to pain seems almost unnatural, 'the more it is hurt the harder it bites'. Yet the traditional bulldog, the sort characterised by the painting of Crib and Rosa painted by Abraham Cooper in 1813, was ideal for the bear pit but a shade slow for dog fighting. Hence a faster, equally hard biting dog was developed, namely the bull terrier, though whether or not terrier blood was used to effect the change is debatable. Furthermore, the invasion of the brown rat and the sport of ratting had further affected the change in the bulldog.

Curiously, the strict London Rules that governed these illegal dog-fighting matches were a far cry from the notorious activities of the bear gardens and bull rings. Dogs fought to strict rules, as strict as those imposed on the prize ring by Broughton during the same era, and vaguely similar to the rules that governed the conduct of bare knuckled battles. Prior to the contest dogs were bathed in milk and a man required to taste each dog to ascertain if either dog was daubed in some noxious substance to deter the other dog from biting it. Dogs fought in bursts, crossing the line to fight their opponent, and a dog that failed to cross the line when it was its turn to do so was deemed the loser of the contest. It is said that under these rules it was possible for a dead dog to win a contest if the other dog whose turn it was to cross the line refused to attack the cadaver. Conan Doyle, through the mouth of Brigadier Gerard, refers to the British as 'a most curious race'. Indeed, there is much to substantiate his statement!

However, if the sport of dog fighting was considered ignominious it could not compare with the dog-versus-man battles staged in the Midlands. This was perhaps the most degrading spectacle ever devised and shocked even the onlookers. In 1874 a deformed dwarf known as Brummy, whose claim to fame was that he once devoured a live cat, was matched against a bulldog called Physic, both the antagonists being restrained by straps which allowed them to escape the attentions of the other adversary should they wish to do so. The dwarf Brummy pummelled and bit the dog to submission in a period of time described by the *Daily Telegraph* as ten and a half rounds. Brummy was horribly disfigured as a result of the battle and so also was his antagonist who was beaten and bitten unconscious. Such a spectacle was staged at Hanley and drawn by Alfred Cancannen who witnessed the outrage.

A similar contest referred to as an 'arbite' in the report of the contest (a delicious euphemism) was staged in an East End club between one James Oxley and the bulldog Crib owned by Robert Green. Oxley was unlucky. For twenty-one minutes he bludgeoned the dog with his fists before the dog tore off his right ear and swallowed it!

However, in other countries less bizarre and less bloody than Britain, the mastiff types were evolving along different lines – more peaceable lines, perhaps. In Germany a leaner, taller type of mastiff, the Ulmer mastiff, had evolved, thought by many to be an intermediate between the Irish or some other tall Celtic greyhound and a true mastiff. This type, bred originally to hunt boar (one of the most formidable of foes), was often hunted 'in armour' – leather patches which would resist the awesome thrusts of the boar's tusks. The breed was to be referred to as the Great Dane, though the breed has little connection with Denmark. Breeders of this huge mastiff sometimes state that while their dogs are often indifferent to sheep they are often furiously antipathetic to domesticated pigs.

In the Pyrenees a more hirsute type of mastiff with pronounced dew claws had evolved – a shepherd dog which was supposedly responsible for the extinction of the wolf in the Pyrenees. This type of mastiff lived a frugal life, as frugal as the life of the shepherds who bred the dogs, and despite the giant size, these dogs will exist on collie-sized rations of a low protein food. This type of mastiff would later be referred to as the Pyrenean mountain dog and breeders still continue to perpetuate the outlandish dew claws which serve no useful purpose but were supposed to assist the dog in scrabbling up rocky slopes This is clearly ludicrous for such dew claws, vestigial toes which have been bred out in most other breeds, are an inconvenience rather than of any assistance to a dog. Dogs of the Pyrenean mountain dog type, long-coated mastiffs, often travelled on fishing boats to Newfoundland. These fishing boats, often huge flat-bottomed dories, were towed behind the mother ships. Dogs of this type were used to snap up huge cod which flailed around the decks of these dories, and to carry messages between ships – an easily taught skill despite the apparent complexity of the task. In fact it is simplicity itself to teach a dog that displays a natural propensity for water to retrieve buoy ropes.

Carson Ritchie, in *The British Dog*, suggests that these mastiff-type dogs swam ashore and mated with Beothuk dogs (the Beothuk were probably a hybrid Eskimo/Amerindian race who wore body armour of bone strips when engaging in battle and who spoke an Indian dialect liberally sprinkled with Inuit expressions and phrases). These Beothuk dogs were probably husky or Eskimo-type curs and were almost certainly spitz-type. From the union of these Eskimo dogs with the southern mastiff was to emerge the most versatile of dogs – the Newfoundland – and possibly the Labrador retriever, for this breed also originated in Newfoundland, not in nearby Labrador.

The breed was originally used as a draught animal and had a pulling power of a small malemute, yet was definitely more biddable. Many of the earliest photographs of sled dogs do in fact depict Newfoundlands (or dogs very akin to Newfoundlands) rather than the conventional husky types one associates with sledding.

Of the Newfoundland Edward Jesse once wrote, 'the Newfoundland is docile, capable of strong attachment and is easy to please with the quality of its food as he will live on scraps of boiled fish [the customary fare of huskies at the time] either salted or fresh and on boiled potatoes and cabbage.' It is strange that the Pyrenean-type mastiffs all seem to be able to live on the most frugal of diets and survive conditions which would destroy the physique of other dogs.

Like its Basque ancestor, the Newfoundland retained its propensity for water and was often used as a ship's dog, a dog required to take to the water for sundry reasons should its owner require it to do so. The author Robert Michael Ballantyne encountered one of these huge dogs during a visit to Canada; he then used the breed as the eponymous hero of his best-selling children's book *The Dog Crusoe* – though the book is possibly too anthropomorphic to please the average twelve-year-old reader. Crusoe has all the qualities of a canine super-hero – he is brave, strong and above all incredibly loyal. Small wonder the breed became so popular in Britain.

So popular was the Newfoundland and so docile its disposition that it achieved the rather unwanted title 'The Most Stolen Dog in Britain' in the latter part of the nineteenth century. The reader may forgive a slight diversion, for the subject of dog thieves should not pass unmentioned in a book of this kind. During the nineteenth century dog stealing became such a common event that it was quite a problem in the cities. Mayhew, in *London Labour, London Poor* (1862), condemns these thieves in a particularly damning manner, 'Dog stealing is very prevalent, particularly in the West End of the Metropolis and is rather a profitable form of felony. These thieves reside at Seven Dials in the neighbourhood of Belgravia, Chelsea, Knightsbridge and low neighbourhoods, some of them of mature years'.

Mayhew tended to classify humanity much in the same manner as Linnaeus had classified flora and fauna and continues, 'Sometimes they belong to the felon class, sometimes not. They are often connected to breed fanciers, keepers of fighting dogs and persons who set up rat matches' (which, incidentally, Mayhew enjoyed and visited regularly).

The incredible number of Newfoundlands stolen during this era is fairly easily explained. In addition to the fact that, unlike its mastiff relatives, the breed showed little antipathy to strangers, it was probably the second most popular one in Britain between the time when W.R. Pape staged the first dog show in Britain and the turn of the twentieth century, so it was not surprising that advertisements for Newfoundlands in the 'Lost and Found' columns of the London newspapers were legion. The subject of dog stealing will be dealt with in a later chapter.

It is likely that the Newfoundland shares a common ancestry with the Labrador retriever because both originated in Newfoundland and both are obviously of the brachycephalic or mastiff type. Both share a desire to work in water and both make admirable retrievers – two qualities which sometimes caused dismay among swimmers. A corps of life-saving dogs had been established on the banks of the Seine in Paris – some of which were of Labrador type but the majority of which were clearly Newfoundlands. They were trained for their life-saving duties by encouraging them to fetch straw-filled dummies from the river and for about ten years performed their tasks admirably, but many took their duties so seriously that the dogs insisted on rescuing swimmers who were in no danger of drowning.

Landseer was intrigued by the great strength and beauty of the breed, so intrigued in fact that he painted a picture of a huge pied Newfoundland (considerably lighter in type than the modern Newfoundland) and entitled the painting *A Distinguished Member of the Royal Humane Society* – a society devoted to saving those in danger of drowning. These pied Newfoundlands, less common than the large chocolate brown variety, are still referred to as Landseer Newfoundlands.

Let us conclude these references to the Newfoundland with an account of what was referred to as 'The Newfoundland Murder' by the press in October 1803. It appears that Colonel Montgomery and Captain McNamara RN were riding in Hyde Park with their Newfoundlands running at the horses' heels, when a fight began between the two dogs. The owners parted them and a quarrel broke out between the two officers and, despite the fact that duelling was illegal at this time, they decided that honour could only be satisfied by dint of pistols. McNamara was wounded but Montgomery was killed instantly and the naval officer faced trial for murder.

Part of McNamara's defence was that he was of the Anglo-Irish aristocracy, a social group which despite the law had always settled their problems by duelling, but the character witness in the form of Lord Nelson, whose appearance in the court brought applause from the onlookers and jury alike, probably produced a 'not guilty' verdict from the jury, despite the fact that the judge directed them to find the captain guilty of murder.

The Fiennes also categorise the scent hounds under the heading mastiff type dogs. Indeed, Dunbar describes the bloodhound as the closest relation of the Molossian and Hyrcanian mastiff described by Herodotus. As to the origin of the name bloodhound, many believe it to be a hound used to trail the blood scent of a wounded animal – a deer or bear perhaps. Others believe the hound to be the purest representative of the Talbot or southern hound and hence the term bloodhound might be an appellation meaning a pure-blooded hound. Turberville, however, uses the expression bloodhound to describe a large hound used to hunt otter and it is fairly obvious that at that time the term bloodhound did not apply to a distinct breed of hound, but simply a St Hubert type hound which possessed an extremely good nose.

Modern bloodhounds are the most docile and delightful of hounds, a gentle beast, a dog that is safe with the smallest of children. Yet the breed did not always enjoy such a reputation. It is believed that the hound's man-hunting abilities had been developed by trackers and man-hunters along the Scottish/English borders in the time prior to 1609, when James I became king of both England and Scotland and supposedly the hostilities between the two countries came to an abrupt end. Gisland, in Cumbria, produced some of the finest sleuth hounds – as man-hunting hounds were often referred to in those times – and one of the great man-hunters of the time was John of Lorn who obtained hounds trained on the Esk to hunt down Scottish raiders.

Phillip II of Spain was seemingly fascinated with the scenting ability of bloodhounds and how eagerly they ran the scent of runaway slaves and criminals, and sent several of these hounds to the Americas where they were either bred for sheer ferocity or crossed with some sort of mastiff to confer the desire to come to grips with their quarry – the original hounds often barked joyfully when they found their 'quarry' but never attacked the cornered human. Indeed, John of Lorn endeavoured to secure Wallace's own hounds as he believed they would find their absent master more quickly than would Lorn's hounds. Cuban bloodhounds were, however, a totally different type of dog and displayed furious antipathy to the quarry they hunted.

Whatever the make-up of the Cuban hounds they were the most feared of dogs. At Haut du Cap in Haiti the French tracker Turpin was said to encourage the accentuation of this antipathy in the hounds' tracking ability by feeding his pack a live negro from time to time. Turpin's hounds were also able to distinguish 'blacked up white men' from negroes and were said to fawn at the feet of the imposters but dismember black slaves.

Carson Ritchie, in *The British Dog*, tells an interesting tale of these Cuban hounds. A ship's crew mutinied off the coast of Cuba and murdered their officers and all British hands before disappearing into the mountains of Cuba where in the jungles and scrub they were confident no-one would find them. The Spanish governor of Cuba heard of the mutiny and sent a mere dozen dog handlers to track the mutineers. All the crew were captured and hanged in Havana.

The trainer of these hounds enjoyed a regular salary and great respect. He was required to keep and train at least three hounds, but at home the hounds were kept chained and muzzled. Off the leash and unmuzzled they knew they must attack the quarry with great ferocity.

The bloodhound

Once again to quote Ritchie's research, in 1795 there was a particularly bloody slave rebellion in Jamaica when the white settlers declared war on the Maroons. Maroons were escaped slaves (the word *maroon* means 'wild') who lived in the bushy interior of Cuba, Haiti and Jamaica and who butchered anyone, black or white, who strayed into their domain. Most of them spoke Spanish and were particularly ferocious to the British who were regarded as even more barbarous in their treatment of slaves than the Spanish or French.

The British commander in Jamaica decided that the only way to deal with this rebellion was to hunt down all the Maroons and re-enslave or execute them, so he hired a famous man-hunter called Don Manuel de Sejas, a *chasseur* who specialised in the capture of recalcitrant and dangerous slaves (one can only assume the fate of any slaves De Sejas tracked down). De Sejas and his mercenaries arrived in Kingston but the British commander General Walpole was unimpressed by the hounds, despite the fact that every slave in Kingston ran and hid when the hounds and *chasseurs* left the ship. At Seven Rivers he ordered a review of the dogs and handlers and asked for a demonstration of how the dogs behaved under fire, for many of the Maroons carried firearms. The hounds attacked the stocks of the guns fired by their handlers and Walpole ordered his coachman to leave the scene as the hounds displayed a furious hatred of his coach and horses.

The *chasseur* de Sejas had no opportunity to demonstrate the ability of the hounds, however, for the Maroons, hearing of the scene at Seven Rivers, capitulated and accepted the Governor's terms. The Napoleonic General Boyer kept a small pack of these furious hounds and treated his slaves brutally. If they were insolent they were flogged, sometimes to death, and if they escaped and were captured they were maimed to prevent further escape. When his cook supposedly cheated the General of some two pence, he ordered the wretch to be fed alive to the bloodhounds in the gardens of Government House and invited the slave's family and friends to watch the punishment. Perhaps it is small wonder that L'Ouveture's troops attacked the garrison with such fury when they stormed Government House.

The bloodhound is just one example of the Talbot hound, or St Hubert hound, brought to Britain by the Normans and used to hunt the enormous variety of quarry that lived in Britain at that time. The hounds were divided into two categories, according to Gilbey in *Hounds in the Old Days*: the black or black and tan hound, examples of which are found at the Dumfriesshire Otterhound Kennels and at the Scarteen Foxhound Kennels in Ireland; and the white variety often depicted on the inn signs for the numerous Talbot Arms throughout the country. These white hounds varied in size from great twenty-seven inch beasts capable of killing stags, wolves and perhaps boar, to diminutive hounds kept perhaps more as pets than hunters – so small that 'they might snugly fit in a gentleman's glove'.

The Normans and the Angerins who inherited the British crown kept hounds to hunt deer and hare, and while they were not adverse to a tilt at any living creature, viewed the pursuit of fox and wolf as being slightly demeaning. Yet both the hare and the deer leave a strong scent which dogs of all breeds pursue enthusiastically. Wolves were seldom hunted by the nobility for the quarry exhausted both the hound and the horseman and the extinction of the British wolf must be attributed to traps and poisons – usually the deadly aconite or monkshood referred to by early apothecaries as 'wolfsbane'.

The great staghound now largely confined to the south west of Britain, the fox hound, the harrier and the beagle must be considered as variations of the same breed. Indeed, there is little to distinguish the beagle from the staghound except its size. Each type possessed large, pendulous ears said to help sweep up the scent of the beast the hound is pursuing, and heavy jowls which may further facilitate the hounds' scenting ability – many hounds do in fact appear to drink in the scent rather than simply sniff the scent of the quarry they are hunting.

The largest of this St Hubert or Talbot white hound, the staghound, was developed to have the strength and size to pull down the largest and most testing British quarry, the red deer, specimens of which at one time weighed in at twenty stone, before these deer were forced to quit the great forests of Britain and seek a more harsh and inclement lifestyle on the moorlands of these islands. There is some evidence to suggest that deer reared on the poor pastures of Exmoor, Dartmoor and Sutherland might be considered smaller and less strong than the deer pursued by the hounds in the Royal Forests, areas of arable land set aside by the nobility and allowed to revert to forest once again. Such deer towered above Landseer's *Monarch* and were terrible adversaries if brought to bay by hounds. Williamson's Deadlock, anti-hero of *Tarka the Otter*, was a staghound that had lost its speed after being almost gutted by a stag that had been brought to bay, and the hound had been drafted to hunt otter – a less testing quarry despite the terrible death experienced by Deadlock.

Smaller than the great staghound, but larger than the harrier, is the English foxhound. The pursuit of the fox was considered an inferior sort of sport in Elizabethan and Stuart times – Caius apparently regarded deer and hare as the only quarry to hunt with hounds, and fox as 'an artificial quarry' (Gilbey). But as Jesse points out, Caius should not be regarded as an authority on dogs for he knew little (and cared less) of dogs of any sort. Why fox hunting became a fashionable sport during the eighteenth century can easily be explained, however. Britain's military greatness during this era was not simply due to the expendability of the thin red line (poverty persuaded many men into military service and there was 'always a surplus of soldiery') but to the fact that the British had perfected speedy and efficient attacks achieved by a combination of forced marches by the infantry and stinging charges by a well-mounted cavalry: the relevance of this to fox hunting will be explained later.

The slow-moving southern hound was not really suitable for the pursuit of fox, for while the hare, like the Biblical son of man, had no place to hide its head and hence could be taken by hounds capable of enduring a grinding war of attrition, foxes when pursued by this form of hound simply ran to ground. Thus a faster type of hound was required to catch the fox before it ran to an earth. The improvements to the type of fox hound desired by those who rode to hounds (as opposed to the foot packs, for the fell hounds developed along different lines for different reasons) is credited to that great horseman Hugo Meynell, who produced a faster, more homogenous, more nimble scent hound from the hotch potch of hound types of the time.

Meynell was born at Quondon Hall (later to be shortened to the Quorn in 1735), inheriting the family property in 1753 after a family quarrel caused his older brother to be disinherited, and began his interest in hunting at an early age. Meynell enjoyed the hunt rather than the kill, unlike his predecessors who would run a fox to ground and then dig the beast from a great depth while the field (the other horsemen) were forced to wait nearby at a suitable distance from the earth being dug. In 1687 the second Duke of Buckingham, a man who like Surtees Jorrocks 'always dug', ran a fox to ground in a deep badger sette and took part in a very lengthy dig, despite the fact that most of the field had retired and copious quantities of rain continued to fall. His enthusiasm was met with little reward, for while he unearthed and killed the fox he died of pneumonia a week later.

How Meynell developed a faster, more homogenous hound that still had voice and scenting ability is debatable, but he most certainly used some form of greyhound in its development, later breeding out the sight hound shape but retaining some of the speed of the greyhound. The speed achieved by these new hounds was little short of phenomenal. The jockey capped cripple, Old Lal, driving a cart pulled by foxhounds was capable of outpacing the fastest coaches of the era and travelled great distances at speeds exceeding thirteen miles per hour. The profligate Colonel Thornton, one of the great eccentrics of his day, once owned a foxhound he called Merkin, a hound which ran a four mile course in seven minutes, averaging speeds of 36 miles per hour.

Such an improvement was wrought by Meynell's hounds that he is credited with being a master of eugenics (an improver of stock by careful selection) and by 1820 the majority of the mounted packs of Britain fielded Quorn-bred hounds. It was said that by this date half the hounds of Britain were sired by Meynell's Guzman and the other half by Lord Yarborough's Ranter.

It is of interest to note that before Meynell's transformation of the foxhound, slow native ponies and draught horses were able to keep pace with the foxhounds of the period. However as the speed of the foxhound increased horses were bred to keep pace with these hounds and more and more Arab-blooded horses were used for hunting. The evolution of the modern hunter/thoroughbred was in fact probably triggered by improvements to the foxhound.

Wellesley, the first Duke of Wellington, believed that no better training suited the cavalry officer than a season or so on the hunting field where fiery horses needed to be controlled during the din and fury of a 'run', and, while it is questionable that Waterloo was won on the playing fields of Eton, there is little doubt that the success of the British cavalry during the Napoleonic Wars was due at least in part to the training afforded its officers during fox hunts.

America has produced an amazing variety of scent hounds – July, Bluetick, Redbone, Birdsong etc. – most of which are descended from

English or French foxhounds, sometimes with a liberal sprinkling of bloodhound.

The origin of these hounds is certainly worth mentioning. The native American grey fox affords the horseman a very poor run. The species 'trees' as often as it runs to ground and is so small that only specially bred terriers can creep to ground to bolt them. Hence the American fox-hunting fraternity imported both red foxes and suitable hounds to hunt them.

America, however, boasts a huge variety of heavily scented game – boar, razorback and imported Prussian boar, a great variety of deer, raccoon, possum bear and cougar – all of which would prove a distraction to fox-hunting hounds. Hence the cull rate of early packs must have been staggering and while the majority of these hounds would have been destroyed by the huntsmen, some clearly found their way to settlers after the hounds had started to follow mixed trails (i.e. to hunt non-vulpine game). From these 'foul-running' hounds the various breeds of American hound have been developed.

Fast foxhounds were considered desirable, but speedy harriers were not – at least according to Beckford, who believed it unfair to place the hare in a situation where it might easily be killed. Hence the dichotomy between foxhound and harrier, originally size varieties of the same breed, became yet wider. Taplin gives another reason for the widening of the differences between the two types of hound. Fashion dictated that those who wished to lie in bed might follow harriers, for the hunt took place later in the day. This meant that the scent was usually old before the 'field' began to hunt. Thus hounds which could run a cold (or cooling) scent were favoured by those seeking to hunt the hare. Gervaise Markham (1611) suggests a happier medium perhaps regarding the harrier which might have degenerated to a very slow hound indeed if Taplin's reasons had proven true. 'You shall breed your dogs from the slowest and largest of the Southern hounds and the swiftest and smallest of the West Country Hounds being both male and female approved to be staunch, fair and even running, of perfect scent and not given to lie off or look for advantages.' Markham, a Nottinghamshire man, knew of the powerful northern hound and its inability to climb fences or scale stone walls, qualities which brought about the extinction of this type of hound in a county where improvements in agriculture would only be wrought in a country where fields could be well fenced to exclude stock. Thus Markham's intentions for producing a medium-paced hound which was able to negotiate fences during the hunt.

The diminutive beagle too is but a size variant of the St Hubert, though tiny pocket beagles, minute hounds under twelve inches tall, would be used to hunt rabbits and small vermin perhaps. Mary Queen of Scots owned such a pack and during her frequent incarcerations hunted the pack to rabbits. If the beagle is the smallest of hounds, however, it is

The beagle

most certainly one of the gamest and one with the greatest endurance. Some will hunt until they fall with exhaustion, yet still endeavour to rise and follow the scent they are following, giving tongue as they continue to do so.

This propensity to give tongue certainly interested terrier men, particularly terrier men employed by mounted packs whose members wanted the fox bolted and not simply slain underground. A mounted pack needed a terrier which would bay at the fox and cause it to bolt unharmed, thereby affording the field a view. Therefore a terrier which set about its fox furiously, crippling or killing the fox as a terrier in the foot packs of the Lake District might do, was not desired. To produce game yet vocal terriers beagles were mated to the hardest terriers. The oft-quoted *Memoirs of the Old Charlton Hunt* (1737), an amazing piece of literature, comes most readily to mind:

> Let Terriers small be bred and taught to bay
> When Foxes find an unstopped badgers earth
> To guide the delves where to sink the trench
> Peculiar in their breed to some unknown
> Who choose a fighting biting cur who lies
> And is scarce heard but often kills the fox
> With such a one bid him a beagle join
> The smallest kind my nymphs for hare do use
> That cross gives nose and wisdom to come in
> When foxes earth and hounds all baying stand.

One must assume that the nymphs mentioned in this piece of rhyming wisdom were the diminutive pocket beagles 'small enough to fit in a man's glove', or the type of hound mentioned by Taplin which were eleven inches tall and would still run a hare for as long as six hours. A pack of these pocket beagles were, according to Gilbey, owned by a Mr Crane in the 1850s. They measured a mere nine inches at the shoulder and were identically coloured and marked.

Just as the incredible Hugo Meynell was responsible for the improvement in the type of foxhound hunted by mounted followers, so the beagle has been improved by Mr Courtney Williams of the Warwickshire Beagles and Sir Newton Ryecroft MFH, then Master of the Dummer. By dint of selective breeding, without recourse to outcrossing to other breeds of dog, these gentlemen developed the beagle to the type one sees today – a miniature foxhound with great speed and no loss of nose. Just as Meynell's Guzman influenced the development of the modern foxhound, so Dummerwoldsman (1941) changed the course of beagle breeding. Pocket beagles became virtually extinct after this time, though the type levelled out at 14 inches at the shoulder due partly to the influence exerted by this prepotent hound.

The Welsh hound, a quarrelsome, hard-biting, rough-coated beast, similar to the otter hound with which it was sometimes mated to provide new blood, is a curious creature. Supposedly the beast is the result of mating old Celtic or British hounds bred to hunt wolf and boar, if not fox, with hounds from the Ardennes, possibly from St Hubert Abbey, and blending in hounds from the Old North Devon Staghound pack (the pack was eventually sold to Germany, but one and a half couple were reportedly sold to Parson Jack Russell, who in turn sold them to John Dillwyn Llewelyn). Gilbey suggests that these staghounds gave the Welsh hound substance and produced the odd giant hound that occurs in certain packs of purebred Welsh hounds. Most Welsh hounds are smaller and lighter than English foxhounds, however, possibly because the Welsh hound is required to negotiate more hilly, uneven ground than its English counterpart. So uneven is the ground that no horse could follow the hounds in some places and the hounds must find and catch their foxes without help from the huntsmen. The conditions under which these hounds hunt may also make Welsh hounds more independent and difficult to control than the English foxhound.

It would be impossible to conclude a chapter concerned with mastiffs and scent hounds without referring to that curious-looking hound, the dachshund, possibly the most unlikely descendant of *Canis lupus laniger* or the Tibetan wolf. The dachshund is a true hound yet in its native Germany is required to perform the work of a terrier. This is not as unlikely as it appears for most English or Welsh terriers certainly owe their origins to small hounds and Turberville describes terriers (which he refers to as bassets) which must have been virtually identical to dachshunds, even to the mention of the crooked legs sported by this Teutonic hound.

Yet despite its comical appearance the dachshund is a very versatile and useful hound. As the name implies, the dog was first and foremost a hound which was required to go to ground in a badger sette, corner the badger in one of the blind-ended stops and by dint of barking hold the beast at bay until the diggers could delve to the antagonists. No small dog is capable of outmatching a badger so the dog must display all the sense described in that fount of wisdom *Memoirs of the Old Charlton Hunt*, including knowing how to keep a badger at bay by barking rather than biting, for the retaliatory strike of a badger is awesome and damaging.

Smaller types of dachshund, miniature dachshunds, are worked to rabbit, fulfilling the functions of a ferret as much as a terrier, for few dogs are capable of following a rabbit into the galleries of a burrow. There are in fact aficionados of the miniature dachshund in Germany, America and Britain. Teddy Moritz, the American Diana as she is often referred to in the sporting periodicals, hunts rats, rabbits, raccoon, possum and groundhog with her miniature dachshunds and finds them far more versatile than terriers. They are small enough to be able to 'work close to groundhogs yet brave enough to face down a raccoon'.

Larger dachshunds, so-called standard dachshunds, are equally versatile. Garrick Hawkes, the British aficionado of the type, works a variety of quarry with his small hounds and states that, while he finds they are perhaps not as game as some British terriers, they have excellent noses and can be used for a variety of tasks. Dr Brunner, a German sportsman writing in 1979, states that not only will his dogs flush winged game and are passable retrievers, but he has seen them hunt and bring wild boar to bay. Brunner also mentions that rats, rabbits and moorhen often fall victim to his small team of hounds.

At this point it is perhaps expedient to leave the subject of the dogs Fiennes and Fiennes believe to be descended from the awesome Tibetan wolf and discuss the greyhound type of dog supposedly descended from the pale-footed wolf *Canis lupus pallipes* or perhaps the smaller, slighter *Canis lupus arabs*, the Arabian wolf.

The Greyhound Group

There is only the most superficial resemblance between the various greyhound types and the pale-footed or Arabian wolf, yet cynologists of the quality of Zeuner and the Fiennes have not the slightest shadow of doubt that the fleet-footed greyhounds-like dogs are descended from these Asiatic wolves. Yet if wolves are the ancestors of these sight hounds, or greyhound-type dogs, it is possible that other types of wolf may well have given rise to certain types of sight hound. There can often be quite a considerable variation in any litter of wolves of any species. Telman, in *Polyphyletic Origins*, mentions that when he examined a series of litters bred by ten pairs of captive European wolves he found cubs with cranial structures ranging from brachycephalic through mesocephalic to dolichocephalic – sometimes in the same litters. It would only be a matter of time – and a surprisingly short period of time at that – for any primitive race to produce fleet sight-hound types of dog from any species of wild canine, simply by dint of breeding from the fastest, most slender animals. This process of selection might well be unintentional, for hunters would certainly tend to favour the more successful hounds and give these hounds favourable treatment – such as better food and a better place to shelter from the elements. Hence the changes of survival of these fleet, efficient animals would have been greatly increased through such favourable treatment, and the successful dog would have a greater chance of perpetuating its type in the indiscriminate breeding system that exists amongst camp curs of any type.

It is quite amazing that the majority of cynologists seem to insist that the greyhound type first appeared in ancient Egypt and offer the fact that greyhound-type dogs are depicted in some of the tombs of the Egyptian nobility as proof of this theory. It seems highly unlikely that the greyhound type would have been propagated in the conditions that existed in Egypt in the pre-dynastic times, and by the time lithe, slender animals were depicted on the walls of the tombs Egypt was involved in trade with many countries which could have produced this type of dog. It can even be questioned that these lithe, slender dogs are of sight hound type for they may equally well be Niam Niam type dogs which still exist in the Congo and which the Fiennes believe to be descended from dingoes rather than from pale-footed or Arabian wolves.

Their theories concerning the origin of the sight hounds may be considered:

(a) that the type originated in the Middle East and were taken throughout the Old World by traders;
(b) the type originated in central Asia and was taken to Egypt as trade goods;
(c) the type originated independently in the Levant, central Asia and central Europe and hence three distinct types of sight hound may exist and these types may only be distantly or slightly related.

It is possible that the Celtic greyhound group originated abroad from central Europe to southern Russia and spread to the rest of Europe by the successive invasions by certain types of Celt. This type of hound includes the Italian greyhound, the whippet, the track coursing and exhibition greyhound, the Scottish deerhound and the ancestor of the Irish wolfhound, the giant Celtic hound, a colossal beast which according to Carson Ritchie in *The British Dog* may have measured 48 inches at the shoulder and would have towered over the largest Irish wolfhound of today. Walsh and Lowe in *The English Whippet* suggest these breeds, now very different from one another, may well be simply size variations of the same breed.

Italian greyhounds, diminutive little dogs much smaller than the smallest whippets, still retain their desire to chase and if not carefully trained can become bad cat killers, despite their small size and very fragile appearance. These dogs are certainly Jekyll and Hyde personalities. Generations of breeding simply for the pet market, for the breed enjoys toy dog status, have not extinguished the breed's desire to chase and have only dulled their hunting instinct. Many will pursue rabbits and hares with great enthusiasm and follow their rabbits and foxes to ground. A pair kept in the suburbs of a large city became the cause of some controversy when they created a din tackling foxes which made nocturnal forays into the garden to which the pair of Italian greyhounds had constant access. Some of these tiny hounds are deceptively brave despite their 'nesh' mannerisms.

Whippets are slightly larger than the toy-like Italian greyhounds and are usually extremely game little dogs. The breed is amazingly robust and hardy despite its fragile shape. Some are fast enough to come to terms with hare, but the whippet is essentially a rabbit-hunting dog and excels at a short sharp dash, with rapid acceleration over 25 yards or so, and as few rabbits feed far from home during daylight hours the whippet is specifically geared to deal with this type of quarry. Hares are usually too strong and fleet for these tiny hounds to catch, though some learn to come to terms with the strongest brown hares.

The origin of the whippet is shrouded in mystery. It is possibly a bred-down greyhound, a type produced by breeding from small greyhounds and keeping the smallest of the offspring to perpetuate the line. Likewise the type may have originated by crossing terriers with greyhounds, the progeny being used for the unsavoury sport of rabbit coursing, and here the reader must forgive a slight digression while the expression 'rabbit coursing' is explained. Rabbit coursing was a travesty that bears little resemblance to conventional coursing and consisted of turning loose captive wild rabbits in an enclosure from which the rabbits had little chance of escaping. As there was a superabundance of rabbits at the turn of the century, when this nasty little activity achieved some notoriety, some thirty-one rabbits were placed forty or fifty yards from the dogs and the dogs then slipped at the rabbits as soon as the wretched creatures were released.

Wild rabbits released off territory will either run wildly, fear increasing their chances of being captured or else squat in the hope of being overlooked by their pursuers. Dogs which were required to run a succession of released rabbits tired rapidly and the prize was given to the dog that could catch the greatest number of rabbits out of the thirty-one hapless victims released before it. It was a brutal and pointless exercise and one which should never be confused with legitimate hunting.

This barbaric practise should have been brought to an end by the 1911 Protection of Animals Act which effectively outlawed the rat pits, but rabbit coursing continued until 1912 when the Waters versus Meakin case highlighted the barbarism of the activity and showed that there had been considerable cruelty and unnecessary suffering caused by the pastime. In 1921 an amendment to the 1911 Act was passed which specifically made it an offence to course or hunt animals in an enclosed space from which they had no reasonable chance of escaping.

At first leggy terriers were the participants in this foul sport, but soon greyhound blood was brought in to produce more speedy animals which could catch the rabbits more quickly. From this union of terrier and greyhound blood the whippet may have arisen and also the Manchester terrier which has a decidedly sight hound-type appearance.

Whippet racing also tended to refine the shape of the whippet at first, though after World War II a revival in the sport found the conventional Kennel Club registered whippets lacking in both speed and inclination to chase a mechanical lure. Hence more track and coursing greyhound blood was introduced into the strains of racing whippet until now two types of whippet exist: the typical KC registered roach-backed whippet and the track whippet which races under BWRA rules and lack the characteristic shape of KC registered whippets.

The greyhound is often awarded the appellation 'the most ancient of breeds', but this statement is based on the premise that the sleeky-shaped types of dogs depicted on the tombs in the Valley of the Kings actually were greyhounds. In all probability the greyhound was brought to Britain by Celtic invaders and existed in a variety of forms until coursing clubs were formed to improve the hare coursing ability of these hounds. Some of the finest early coursing runners were smooth-coated

The greyhound

and judicious line breeding to these hounds eradicated the rough coat which characterised some of the strains of seventeenth- and eighteenth-century greyhounds. There is a belief that the smooth coat of the greyhound and its brindle coloration was the result of the eccentric Lord Orford crossing the greyhound with the bulldog to increase the courage of the former, but by the time Orford's dogs made an impact on the coursing scene and were offered at public stud by Orford's successor, Colonel Thornton, the bulldog blood was so diluted as to be of little consequence. It is of interest to note that Orford was a dabbler in genetics, a meddler who pursued not a distinct goal but mated a variety of dogs to his coursing greyhounds, including lurchers and Italian greyhounds, in his experiments. His contribution to canine eugenics was slight and he pales to insignificance when compared to stockmen of the calibre of Hugo Meynell.

Greyhounds once hunted a variety of quarry ranging from deer to wolf and hare but curiously many greyhounds show little antipathy to foxes. In that early sporting epic *Master of the Game*, penned in the years 1406–1413, we read 'a little greyhound is very hardy when he takes a fox by himself for men have seen great greyhounds which might well take a hare and a wild boar and a wolf and would let a fox go'.

The traditional prey of the greyhound is the brown hare, the greatest mammalian athlete in the world, and the coursing of this creature is the most testing of sports for the hound. Hares are allowed a start of perhaps 80 to 100 yards (the advantage being termed 'law') before a pair of hounds are slipped at the hare and the prize is awarded to the dog that works best to secure the possible capture of the hare. Few hares are captured, even by a strong pair of fleet hounds, for the hare is a wonderful piece of organic engineering.

In 1926 the sport of greyhound racing began, though whippet racing with strict codes of conduct and very meticulous rules had existed for half a century before this time. Whippets were required to chase a rag and in the early days thrown towards the rag by a trainer or slipper.

Greyhound racing is a far more spectacular affair, however, and involves the hounds being released from mechanically operated boxes to pursue a mechanical hare. There is evidence that greyhound racing accelerated the improvement of the greyhound in a manner than neither Thornton nor Orford could ever imagine. The track heroes of yesterday, such as the renowned Mick the Miller, would be regarded as a joke if their times were to be compared with those of modern Derby and St Leger winners. In fact there are lurcher and long-dog composites, admittedly bred in part from greyhounds, which produce times to better those of early track heroes.

Scottish deerhounds are simply large, long-haired greyhounds – in fact one of the earliest standards for the breed suggests that the deerhound should be 'a large hirsute greyhound'. The Scottish deerhound is perhaps the purest form of the now extinct great Irish hound and towers above all but the tallest greyhounds.

Originally the deerhound was used to hunt wolf, boar, fox and particularly the red deer, and it usually required two of these superb hounds to course and capture a red deer stag which when brought to bay can be a terrible adversary. Occasionally a single hound would be able to pull down a stag but these super hounds were so uncommon that they entered into the poetry of the Gael. Wolf also fell prey to these hounds which were the only type of dog fast enough to come to terms with the wolf. Most of the later wolf hunts in the Highlands involved the use of such hounds. The half-witted macabre McQueen, last of the great Scottish wolf hunters, used such a dog to slay one of the last wolves in Britain, though it is said that wolves still inhabited certain remote areas of Ireland long after this time.

However, the Napoleonic wars saw the decline of this great hound. Improvements in military musketry were copied by manufacturers of sporting guns and it became possible to shoot the wily red deer from a great distance. Hence deerstalking replaced deer coursing as the entertainment of the sporting aristocracy. The great deerhound was relegated to the role of the deerstalker's dog, a hound required only to track wounded deer and by dint of barking bring it to bay – a task more fitting to a collie mongrel than a majestic thirty inch hound.

The deerhound of today is seldom put to appropriate use, for the pursuit of deer with any sort of dog is illegal in Scotland, one of the last

The Irish wolfhound

places where truly wild deer could possibly be coursed, but the Deerhound Club still holds coursing meets near Inverness – which it shares with the Saluki Coursing Club. The quarry is the blue hare, a beast which, while it lacks the athletic ability of the brown hare, makes admirable use of the country in which it lives and will bring a pursuer to grief by affecting its escape over peat hag and rock scree.

The fifth member of the Celtic greyhound clan is the Irish wolfhound – truly a canine enigma. It is said that the great Celtic hound had become extinct long before Captain G.A. Graham started to revive the breed in 1862 and what specimens did exist were a far cry from the great hounds of yore. To revive the breed, or to perhaps recreate the breed, Captain Graham bought up the sorry specimens purported to be Irish wolfhounds and mated them to the best Scottish deerhounds he could obtain. The result of this cross is questionable and Graham considered the progeny of these matings to be too greyhoundy to be considered as typical Irish wolfhounds – though the great Irish wolfhound must certainly have been a huge hirsute greyhound rather than the heavy, powerful but slow-moving beasts we refer to as Irish wolfhounds today. Later, to give the new breed substance, Graham mated mastiffs, Great Danes (probably descendants of the great Irish hounds and heavier mastiff types) and an unknown breed Graham refers to as a Tibetan dog – which was probably an exotic title for a large, powerful, heavy dog of unknown origin but measuring 33 inches at the shoulder. Graham obtained the latter beast from a London livestock producer who specialised in selling curious types

A lurcher

of dog. Conan Doyle certainly knew of the tale and afforded the fearsome Hound of the Baskervilles a similar origin. Later to refine the breed Graham is also reputed to have used a borzoi cross using a hound called Korotai which appears in the pedigree of certain deerhounds.

The Irish wolfhound of today is a far cry from the great Irish greyhound described by Taplin and illustrated by J.G. Woods. The modern beast is too heavy and suffers from certain hereditary faults as a result of its great weight and size. Few of these giant hounds seem to live to the great age one expects of a greyhound and an eight-year-old wolfhound usually looks decidedly antique. Lest the reader quote the fact that the great hound mentioned by Carson Ritchie in *The British Dog* was possibly 48 inches at the shoulder, a good head taller than the modern Irish wolfhound, let us remember that the great Irish hound was a large, rough-coated greyhound and not the hirsute mastiff type we see today. Breeders would do well to remember that if the breed is to continue and to become even taller than it is today, then the type must be fined down to a shape akin to that of the greyhound and become a dog that is still capable of coursing a wolf or pulling down a stag. If height is to be increased then girth must not, for the Irish wolfhound is a far cry from the athletic great Irish hound of yesteryear.

It would be impossible to leave the subject of the Celtic hound without mentioning the lurcher and the long-dog, for at the time of writing it is possible that the lurcher is the most popular breed of dog in Britain today.

Traditionally lurchers are hybrids between sight hounds and some type of herding dog, the object of such cross-breeding being to produce a speedy type of hunting dog with the sagacity and tractability of the herding dog. The lurcher is a relatively new type of cross-breed and has only started to become numerous since rabbits became plentiful in the British countryside. Rabbits are indeed the traditional quarry of the lurcher, though many show a marked propensity to hunt feathered quarry. It is a mistake to imagine that the best hunters are greyhound-saturated hybrids and are valued more highly because of their great speed. Lurchers are prized for their versatility and their ability to hunt up and find quarry rather than for their sheer velocity.

Long-dogs are, or rather should be, quite distinct from lurchers. Long-dogs are hybrids between certain sight hounds, deerhounds x greyhounds, saluki x greyhound, whippet x greyhound and so on and are bred specifically to chase hares. In theory these hybrids should have the speed of a greyhound and the extra stamina conferred by a dash of another breed of sight hound. This enables the type to continue a course long after a greyhound would be spent and to possibly catch a hare, even a hare that has been afforded the 80–100 yards law. Yet the hare is an astounding athlete, a creature that is capable of outrunning most of its pursuers and it is an exceptional dog that can course and catch a hare that has been allowed great law. Tales of super-dogs which are capable of catching five out of every six hares they run are legion. Readers should treat such tales with caution for they are usually lies – silly tales few experienced coursers bother to heed. These tales are made yet more ridiculous by the fact that during the Waterloo Cup, a prize for which the best greyhounds compete, few hares are captured despite the fact that two of the best conditioned greyhounds in the world are chasing them. A long-dog is usually run singly at its hare and the maximum law (100 yards) is usually given to the hare. It is the most exceptional of hounds that can capture a hare under such conditions and few long-dogs are capable of consistently good performances against strong winter hares. Hares are not particularly testing for a long-dog in the early autumn when the young and foolish hares are fairly easily captured. However, by Christmas only the strongest and most alert hares have survived the heavy cull exacted by winter and hence the major coursing events are run in January or early February when dogs are tested against the strongest and best hares – and both greyhounds and long-dogs are usually bested when matched against such winter hares.

Of the middle eastern sight hounds the saluki and the Afghan hound are the best-known of these breeds and both are required to hunt the same type of quarry – gazelles, hares and small deer. Indeed, it is often debated as to whether the Afghan hound is simply a very hirsute saluki or if the saluki is really a smooth-coated form of the Afghan hound. Clearly both types are related and are bred from a common stock. Both

The Afghan hound

The saluki or desert greyhound

the saluki and the Afghan hound are recalcitrant and difficult to train to a high standard – at least by conventional training methods – and both hounds run with a curious loping style which is distinct from the running style of Celtic greyhounds. Both the Afghan hound and the saluki are tailored for long distance running. Indeed courses of three miles have been recorded when salukis run hares and such courses would exhaust or kill a greyhound which attempted such a run.

Both the Afghan hound and the saluki are trained to take part in a curious hunting technique known as 'chirk hawking'. When hounds are matched against a quarry that is not only strong and swift but too wily to approach so as to afford the hounds a reasonable 'slip', hawks are used to slow up or baffle the quarry.

Afghan hounds are run at the chinkara, a small fleet deer that has an amazing acceleration and of whom the Afghans say:

> On the day it is born a man might catch it
> On the second day, a swift hound
> But on the third day – Allah.

To catch such a fleet animal a large and powerful goshawk is taken from its nest when young and trained to feed only on the stuffed head of a chinkara. Later the stuffed body of a deer is towed behind a horse and strips of meat affixed to the head of the stuffed deer. When the hawk is thoroughly used to such a practice it is flown at a live chinkara and, expecting to find meat between the horns of the deer, stoops at the head of the creature and confuses and baffles the deer until a hound can come to grips with it.

Salukis are trained to work with similarly trained saker falcons to capture the fleet Arabian gazelle, though no Afghan and only one Bedouin chieftain still trains this unique combination of dog and hawk.

It is interesting to note that Jack Mavrodagato also used a hound/hawk combination (a greyhound and a gos hawk) to capture brown hares but Mavrodagato considered it an unsporting practice.

Of the origin of the borzoi it is difficult to ascertain whether the dog is of Asiatic or Celtic origin or perhaps an intermediate form. Tale has it that saluki-type dogs were taken with Tartar or Turkish settlers and mated with northern shepherd or guard dogs and produced these giant Russian wolfhounds. However it is equally likely that the borzoi – the name means 'swift' – is a descendant of Celtic hounds shipped from Britain to Poland and thence to Russia. It may also be the result of mating together Celtic and middle eastern hounds.

This huge dog, as tall as the largest deerhound, was at one time used to catch and kill the Palaearctic wolf and prior to the Russian Revolution huge kennels of these hounds were kept by the Russian aristocracy. These hounds were, in the latter days of the Romanoffs, not only status symbols but quite an important source of income to the boyars who bred these hounds. The Perchino kennels often advertised both trained hounds and puppies in America in *Field and Stream*.

These great kennels were destroyed by the revolutionary troops who regarded these hounds as symbolic of the decadent Russian aristocracy and destroyed these dogs often with great fury. Thus for many years the borzoi apparently vanished from its native land. However, in the last thirty years there is evidence to suggest that fur hunters south of the Taiga are still using these borzois, dogs very similar to the beautiful Perchino hounds, to capture foxes, for the pelts of these animals are scarcely damaged by these hounds and are worth considerably more than the pelts of foxes that fall victim to the steel traps.

The Mediterranean hounds, the Pharaoh hound and the larger Ibizan hounds, are probably descended from either Celtic greyhounds taken south by the Celtic Gauls, or perhaps the migrating Vandals who colonised both Spain and the shores of north Africa, or middle eastern hounds brought north by the invading Muslims. It is also believed that both these hounds, which are very similar in type and disposition, could be the result of mating Celtic and middle eastern sight hounds with native curs.

These hounds are kept primarily for rabbit hunting – indeed the Balearic islands may well be the original home of the European rabbit – and are used in much the same way as the British lurcher. The Pharaoh hound, a native of Malta despite its title, is the only vocal sight hound. As a rule sight hounds hunt silently but this Maltese hound indicates the presence of rabbits in the dry-stone walls that criss-cross the island by barking and the rabbit hunter then nets the wall and flushes the rabbit with a ferret.

Sight hounds are scarcely the most intelligent of canines and are slow to learn rudimentary obedience. Their marked propensity to chase also renders them a liability if the hounds are untrained. Sadly the regal demeanour and exotic appearance of many of these hounds does tend to attract the wrong sort of owner and hence the cup of the breed rescue societies overfloweth. It is a trifle unfair for those with little interest in (or an antipathy to) the chase to own one of these hounds and to expect them to desist from hunting – it is not only unfair but little short of impossible to curb this instinct. Salukis show an instant interest in hares, borzois are very antipathetic to foxes and few deerhounds are not motivated by the bobbing white rear of a roe deer.

It has been suggested that sight hounds, or rather the ancestors of sight hounds, have been domesticated for perhaps twenty thousand years. To eradicate this interest in the chase in a single generation is virtually impossible and potential buyers should learn much about these hounds before affecting a purchase.

The Dingo Group

This classification is quite a loose one and the Fiennes believe it is possible that the dingo, like the sight hounds, is descended from the pale-footed Asian wolf *Canis lupus pallipes*. However, the dingo group is one into which the Fiennes seem to place a variety of canine oddities. Enough has been said of the dingo earlier in this book, except to say that similar types of dog are to be found in New Guinea though the Melensian dogs are less homogenous than the Australian dingo – possibly because European settlers have introduced other breeds of dog to New Guinea and these have mated with the native dingo-type dogs. Yet the New Guinea dingo type is still a fine hunter with an excellent nose and is used primarily as a dog to hunt the tree kangaroo. Legend has it that in the beginning of time when all animals were living in harmony the tree kangaroo ran and hid in the jungle, urging man and dog to play some version of the hide and seek game. Man hid his eyes but Dog was unable to do so and detected where the tree Kangaroo hid. Hence while Man finds it difficult to find the tree Kangaroo, Dog is always able to detect the presence of the animal.

The Fiennes place the basenji and the Niam Niam in this group. Both breeds closely resemble the spitz-tailed dogs depicted on the tombs of ancient Egypt and if any breed of dog deserves the appellation 'the oldest breed in the world', perhaps it should be awarded to the basenji and the Niam Niam. These are the most curious of dogs and when the basenji was first introduced to Britain it was awarded the title 'the barkless dog', for the cry made by this hound resembles the sound of a squeaky door closing or a Swiss goatherd signalling across an alpine valley. However this title was short lived for it was discovered that basenjis living with other dogs soon learned to bark in exactly the same way as normal canines.

The hunting ability of these hounds is very strong and many will point birds or game from a great distance. The breed received a shot in the arm popularity-wise when the film *Goodbye My Lady* was produced. In this rather sickly-sweet tear jerker, a basenji 'Isis of the Blue Nile' escapes its owners and teams up with a semi-literate backwoodsman's son. Together the pair confound the trial-bred Llewellyn setters and pointers alike with the basenji's phenomenal quail scenting ability, but the publicity the dog's ability causes attracts the rightful owners who are concerned that the dog has eaten the low-grade food eaten by the

The basenji

The Rhodesian ridgeback

backwoodsman's family! Yet the lack of tractability of this breed makes it an unsatisfactory bird dog, though its primitive hunting instinct has not been blunted by civilisation.

The Fiennes also place the Rhodesian ridgeback amongst the dingo-class dogs, though this curious hound bears little resemblance to the smaller, curled-tailed basenji. The ridgeback is unique in as much as it has a ridge of hair running contrary to the lie of the coat. During the Boer War it became the symbol of the Afrikaner, the Dutch-speaking farmers of South Africa, in much the same way as the bulldog was said to be symbolic of the British. The origin of the breed is obscure but it is said to be descended from a native Kaffer dog mated to various hounds and mastiff types imported by European settlers.

The hound's great hunting ability and dauntless courage endeared it to the European settlers but no-one was more enthusiastic about the breed than the novelist John Buchan. Buchan had served as private secretary to Lord Milner, High Commissioner for South Africa from 1901 to 1903, and obviously encountered the Boer hunting dog during his stay in South Africa. In 1910 he penned *Prester John*, a fast-moving tale of an attempted coloured rebellion in the Cape and his canine hero was a Rhodesian ridgeback (Buchan describes but does not name the breed) called Colin. The dog has all the attributes Buchan admires: it is courageous, loyal, has a wonderful hunting instinct but suffers a heroic death as a result of its extreme loyalty to the hero of the tale.

The publicity this book gave the breed increased its popularity greatly, though it was only in the 1950s when the book became compulsory reading for certain secondary schools that it boosted the breeding of the type.

Thus the breed types and the behaviour that must be expected of the various breeds. Let us now examine the way the Kennel Club has further influenced the development of the described breeds – for good or perhaps for ill.

The Influence of the Kennel Club on the Development of Breeds of Dog

An Irish wolfhound crippled with a hip disorder, limping pitifully, old before its time. A cocker spaniel crazed with fear and behaving irrationally in bright light. A German shepherd dog, one of the most noble of animals, frothing and rolling in the throes of an epileptic fit. A chow chow, eyes constantly producing a surfeit of tears which stain the fur of the face. An English bulldog, once the symbol of British tenacity, courage and endurance but now a pathetic, wheezing travesty of a beast, entering the world by Caesarian section, leaving it prematurely when heart and lungs finally give up the task of keeping such a blasphemy supplied with air. A bloodhound, once the terrifying hound of de Sejas, the tracker of exiled kings, the scourge of fear-scented law-breakers but now a beast with jowls so heavy that the dog's eye sockets are almost visible. Abominations of animals, hideous examples of how breeding has gone sadly awry – and all the fault of that most nebulous of bodies – the Kennel Club. What utter rubbish, but it is rubbish the man in the street tends to believe, so now perhaps it is expedient to explain the role the Kennel Club has played in the development of the British dog.

If the Regency period was referred to as the Age of Scandal by the scholarly T.H. White, the nineteenth century most certainly merits the title 'The Age of Exhibitions'. In 1851 the Crystal Palace was constructed to house one of the greatest exhibitions of scientific equipment in the history of the world and some twenty years later Paris staged a similar exhibition where British industry fared somewhat less well. However, in 1859 an exhibition that was not only different but epoch making was staged in a small hall in Newcastle on Tyne by the gunmaker W.R. Pape.

Pape's business was experiencing a somewhat difficult period and so to drum up trade and give his firm added publicity he staged the first dog show, which incidentally catered only for pointers and setters – which are classed as gun dogs. To judge this show he appointed J.H. Walsh who wrote copiously, though not particularly exactly, under the pseudonym 'Stonehenge'. Pape's show attracted a number of entries and even greater publicity and months later a show catering only for foxhounds was staged at Redcar, Yorkshire.

In the next few years several small dog shows were staged and in 1863 a really spectacular dog show was run at Ashburnham Hall, Chelsea, a show which catered for many breeds of dog, some of which are now extinct. Two years later constant letters to *The Field* – virtually the only magazine that catered for those who had an interest in dogs – induced certain spaniel, setter and pointer enthusiasts to stage the first field trials at Southill, Bedfordshire and quite suddenly dog breeding became a very profitable business.

Prior to this time dog breeders enjoyed a rather unsavoury reputation. Many were associated with the rat pits, and illegal dog fighting, while others maintained emporia where stolen dogs were held until their owners were prepared to pay the ransom for the return of their pets. Perhaps the reader will forgive the digression, but at this time dog stealing was quite big business. It has already been mentioned that at one time the theft of Newfoundland dogs was extremely profitable, but various other breeds also attracted the attention of professional dog thieves.

Two centuries earlier, Charles II, who showed little interest in the sporting dogs but adored the smaller lap dogs which would eventually be called King Charles spaniels, sat on the throne. Carson Ritchie records that so numerous were these spaniels in the Royal Palace that one of the courtiers once remarked 'God save your majesty, but God damn your dogs'. Yet due to the somewhat lax security of the time, the king's dogs were regularly stolen and sometimes held for ransom and Charles wrote to 'Mercurius Publicus' begging for the return of a cross-breed greyhound (Italian) spaniel which had no value 'except to the King'.

By the mid nineteenth century, however, dog stealing had become a highly sophisticated profession. Elizabeth Barratt Browning wept copiously when her spaniel Flush was stolen and held for ransom. She paid £50 for the return of the dog which apparently lived under permanent threat of the death sentence during its sojourn at her father's house in Wimpole Street.

Dog thieves, again according to Carson Ritchie, adopted two methods of stealing. One was to lure away a dog which was owned by a doting owner by dint of a piece of liver soaked in some secret ingredient which made the meat irresistible to dogs, or if the dog was a male enticing it by walking an in-season bitch near the animal. These thieves would then wait until a reward was offered for the return of the pet and then send an accomplice to negotiate for the return of the animal. If the owner haggled about the price of the settlement the accomplice would then hint darkly at the fate of the dog if the sum asked for was not forthcoming and there are tales of beheaded and mutilated dogs left on the doorsteps of tardy or reluctant payers.

Worse still, some of these dogs fell into the hands of anatomists who, after the publicity body-snatchers received in 1829, were denied the services of Burke and Hare type procurers of human corpses (for parents often sat near the graves of deceased children until the carcasses of these babies decayed enough to confound anatomists) stole or bought stolen pet dogs to use for their vile experiments. Even surgeons of the prominence of Sir Astley Cooper (1768–1841) who was credited with 'raising surgery from its primitive state to a science' was not adverse to luring home someone's pet dog and subjecting the creature to surgery before destroying the now badly maimed animal.

Indeed so sophisticated and common were dog thefts that these activities caused a public outcry. Mayhew, who delighted in seedy places and the disreputable characters of Victorian England, gave the dog thieves much publicity, sometimes during his reign as editor of *Punch* and particularly in his monumental work *London Labour and London Poor* (1851–1862). But a decade before he penned his book, dog stealing had become such a problem that on 26 July 1844 a Select Committee on Dog Stealing submitted a somewhat lengthy and alarming report to the House of Commons which offered no suggestions as to how this problem could be controlled.

Such was the aura that surrounded doggy people at the time when W.R. Pape held what is said to be the first dog show, though animal keepers held 'matches' (competitions of some sort) between cage birds, pet animals, and that curious, delicate enigma the English white terrier in public bars and church halls prior to Pape's first dog show, but once the dog shows became popular further dubious practices were perpetrated.

To win certain classes dogs were dyed, stained and sometimes mutilated to remove certain cosmetic blemishes and the process of 'ringing' (showing dogs under different names or substituting inferior dogs for more desirable animals) became very common. The Victorian critics of dog breeders had described these people as 'doggy men who always seem to congregate in the doorways of clubs' and dog breeders were held in little regard by the public.

To counteract such bad publicity and to monitor the behaviour of certain dog breeders, S.E. Shirley of Warwickshire set up a club to further the exhibiting of dogs and the activities of dog breeders. Thus in 1877 the Kennel Club was formed and soon became to the dog keeper what the Jockey Club had been to the Turf. There had been a stud book to guide the breeding of the foxhound since the days of Hugo Meynell, but now the Kennel Club produced similar stud books for many other breeds of dog and issued a list of rules that should govern the behaviour of breeder and exhibitor alike. As a memory of the more raffish days of dog breeding the Kennel Club also barred any member who had ever 'Welshed' on a bet – shades of Colonel Thornton's days perhaps!

Yet the Kennel Club has neither owned nor bred a single dog and if certain breeds have become deformed by producing their animals purely to win at shows, then it is the breeders of these animals (not the Kennel

Club) who are to blame. Various other canine orientated bodies through Europe have attempted to regulate and govern the breeding of pedigree dogs – in Belgium these bodies have outlawed the practice of line breeding (the process of mating fairly distantly related animals) and certain agencies in Germany have the power to decree to which sires a person must mate his bitches, but no such policy has been adopted by the Kennel Club.

The Kennel Club simply maintains the stud books of various registered breeds of dog and monitors and governs the behaviour of breeders and exhibitors of certain breeds of Kennel Club registered dog. It has certainly never been responsible for deformities and mental abnormalities which have appeared in certain breeds of registered dogs over the years. However, before mentioning the abnormalities that beset certain types of dog, perhaps it is expedient to mention what is normal behaviour in the development of the domesticated dog.

Normal Development of the Dog

In true Dylan Thomas fashion, let us begin at the beginning, and the beginning is obviously the birth of the puppy. Puppies emerge into the world shedding the amnion and the chorion and the other trappings of birth which are invariably eaten by the bitch. The seemingly revolting action is purposeful and is perhaps a reminder of the days when wild dogs nested in subterranean lairs dug by the pregnant female. A bitch which neglected to eat the various sacs and placental attachments of her puppies would soon find her den fouled with decaying tissue which would produce a wonderful culture for harmful bacteria. Hence the bitch eats the trappings of birth, digests the said trappings and passes the remains as a black slimy stool which has a characteristic smell many people find nauseating.

Some schools of thought suggest that a bitch may well ingest her own birth trappings so that she has food enough to last a full twenty-four hours – the critical period in the life of a newly born puppy, and hence does not need to leave her lair or nest box to feed nor allow her puppies to chill. Yet another school of thought suggests that a bitch's milk supply is stimulated and increased by the action of ingesting the amnion, chorion and placental membranes, though it might be difficult to substantiate or disprove such a notion.

The behaviour of bitches at the imminent birth of puppies tells the observer much of the behaviour of the immediate ancestry of a domesticated dog. Bitches seek out privacy when they are ready for parturition and a bitch allowed liberty rather than being confined in a kennel or restricted to a sleeping box will invariably burrow deeply into log piles, waste wood, dry bark or rubbish to produce her litter. Collie bitches allowed to run free around farmsteads will usually attempt to excavate a den to produce young rather than deposit their litter in a secluded but open shed corner. The reasons for this are obvious. Puppies leave the safety and warmth of a bitch's womb, the temperature of which is 101.5°F and emerge often into a world where the temperatures are considerably lower. Hence a young puppy will often chill in the first hours after birth unless the dam has found a crevice that can be warmed by the bitch's body heat. Thus a bitch which is allowed liberty will usually seek out or excavate a small den which can be heated fairly rapidly by her body heat. Farm dogs or rather farm bitches will often excavate several 'dens' before they find one that is suitable and many farm dog owners find it good policy to allow the bitch to give birth in dens they have excavated. If, however, such dens are havens for bacteria it is wise not to allow a bitch to produce puppies in these conditions, for the raw umbilicus of a puppy acts as a gateway through which many dangerous bacteria such as *E. coli* will pass. David Hancock of Sutton Coldfield, the world's largest breeder of lurchers, once owned a red Exmoor collie bitch (a primitive breed of herding dog quite distinct from the border collie), which became extremely distressed if kennelled just prior to parturition. When released from kennels she immediately excavated a deep den under a pile of brushwood and refused to leave the mound of rubbish until she whelped. Her litters were usually reared in perfect comfort in this citadel, even in the depths of winter, and she was never known to lose a puppy through hypothermia. Apparently the bitch had been born in such a den on a remote hill farm on Exmoor, so David Hancock eventually allowed the bitch to whelp where she pleased.

My own bearded collie bitch, Heather, bred from many generations of Grampian shepherd dogs, needs to be watched carefully as she nears parturition. Shortly before the birth of her first litter of puppies in 1986 she disappeared and I scoured the moor behind my croft to find her. After a torrential shower of rain the likes of which only occur in the Highlands, I returned home believing Heather had been drowned in a peat 'cut' – trenches six or seven feet deep from which peat is excavated. Two days later Heather reappeared and virtually asked to be fed. She was heavy in milk, so I assumed she had produced her litter in some rock crevice on the moor, but she became very anxious and suspicious when I attempted to follow her to find her lair on the sodden heathland. Days later I watched Heather wade across the marsh to a burrow of broken concrete slabs where deep inside the mound she had produced two puppies. I failed to reach them and with some trepidation I was forced to leave them there, despite the fact that the downpour continued for the next week and the moor began to resemble a lake. Yet I have never seen better reared puppies and when at three weeks of age they emerged from their lair and I crated them to take them home they showed no sign of any sort of deprivation.

Immediately prior to the bitch's parturition breeders may observe the bitch tearing up the floor of her sleeping box, an action that distresses many newcomers to dog breeding. Bitches will shred newspaper on which they are bedded or actively tear at the fabric of a sleeping box. One of the early saluki breeders who trained soldiers of Glubb Pasha's Arab legion once observed a whelping saluki bitch excavate a deep hole in a mud brick floor before producing her puppies. The purpose of this frantic scratching action has long been debated by cynologists and it is believed that a bitch which undertakes such furious activity stimulates certain glands which produce hormones to facilitate birth. Certainly bitches which are denied an opportunity to perform in such a manner become extremely distressed, although they still produce live healthy puppies.

My own theory concerning the reason for this furious scratching action is both heretical and mundane. I believe that this action is simply a race memory of the time when wild dogs nested and produced young in subterranean lairs. The scratching action creates fine loose soil or even rock dust, for the action is amazingly forceful, and this dust absorbs the foetal fluid which is often produced in copious quantities when certain bitches whelp. Hence puppies are not forced to be born in pools of, albeit sterile, liquid and the mud created when this amniotic fluid mingles with earth soon dries to form an almost mud brick-like surface.

So what can the would-be dog breeder glean from the data I have just offered, or more to the point, how can the dog breeder benefit from the observations of dogs allowed to lead what is loosely referred to as a 'natural' existence? Firstly, while the breeders are wont to whelp bitches in open boxes in full view of the interested family, the majority of bitches usually attempt to seek the seclusion of a cupboard or a similar enclosed area to bear their litter. Not only does a 'lid' reduce heat loss from the newly born litter but the bitch is usually happier to produce her young in private, though the majority of whelping bitches are remarkably tolerant of human interference and allow their owners to handle newly born puppies. A lidded box-like contrivance is usually a more satisfactory nest than an open tray-like affair and when bitches are whelped in the latter it is by no means uncommon to find them carrying their puppies in their mouths, trying to find the seclusion of a dark, warm place within the house.

Scott and Fuller conducted a series of tests in 1962, now known as the Bar Harbour tests (from the town of the same name in Maine). Their experiments advanced the theory that the social development of a dog can be divided into four main categories:

Neonatal or newly born period from birth to 2 weeks of age

Transitional period which begins at 2 weeks and lasts perhaps a week

Socialisation period which commences at 3 weeks

Juvenile period roughly from 10 weeks to 6 months

Adult period which starts at 6 months

When a puppy leaves its dam it is usually enclosed in a foetal sac which might have ruptured during parturition. Often puppies are born completely enclosed in this membrane and the bitch must be very astute at biting through this sac to release the puppy so that it can take its first breath of air. Young bitches are not as diligent at this task as they might be and sometimes dead puppies still enclosed in the sac are found in the whelping boxes of very young bitches which have whelped unexpectedly. Hence the majority of breeders advise firstly never breeding from a bitch during her first season, if that period of sexual activity arrives before the bitch is a year old, for the animal may not be sufficiently mature to perform her parental duties. Secondly they advise attending the bitch while she whelps so that should she be negligent in her duties the breeder can assist her during the birth by tearing open the sac to release a puppy, should the bitch show no inclination to do so.

The bitch will usually lick the puppy vigorously to ensure the whelp is not only free of foetal fluid but has its abdomen and thorax massaged so that the bowels and lungs may be stimulated into functioning. The ancients believed that the ultimate shape of the puppy was determined by the vigour with which the bitch licked her whelps, hence the term 'licking into shape', and it is during this furious period of licking that the puppy takes its first gasps of air. Dunbar suggests that breathing is further stimulated by the bitch licking the puppy's nose and umbilicus, so that mucus is cleared from the nostrils and perhaps the diaphragm is stimulated into action by the cleaning of the umbilicus. This massaging process is very important to the early functions of the whelp and hence astute breeders often keep strips of coarse towelling near to the whelping bitch so that the puppies may be resuscitated by gentle friction should the bitch be negligent in her cleaning of the whelps.

A newly born puppy is equipped with some heat-seeking mechanism and will actively seek out the warmth offered by the bitch. Some may at first try to crawl to the bitch's vagina but in minutes they will normally find a teat and attempt to suckle.

This early suckling period is all important for, during the first few days after parturition, a bitch secretes a yellowy first milk or colostrum, which is not only rich in nutrients but also contains a quantity of the bitch's antibodies which protect a newly born puppy from the sundry infections to which dogs seem heir. This gives immunity lasting perhaps three to six weeks, depending on the level of antibodies in the bitch's colostrum, but after three weeks the immunity conferred tails off and the whelps become less protected from sundry canine ills – this matter will be dealt with presently. However, the puppy also obtains some antibodies across the placental tissue which connects the whelp to its dam before birth so it is possible to rear newly born puppies by hand using a bitch's milk substitute that is deficient in the natural antibodies found in the colostrum.

Puppies are born not only blind, but also deficient in other senses for which the adult dog is famous. They show no response when subjected to sudden sharp noises and bright lights, though Dunbar believes newly born puppies of certain breeds in which the skin is sparsely haired and the eyelids translucent may react to a very strong light. Frankly I have not noticed this to be the case in the short-coated terriers I have bred.

The action of a strong, lusty puppy suckling its dam is fascinating and emotionally satisfying for the breeder to watch. Healthy puppies suckle continuously and may be at the teat actively suckling for as long as two hours a day, furiously pummelling the mammary glands with their forepaws. Cat breeders note that when kittens have selected a particular teat on which to suckle they will suckle only from that teat until they are weaned. Puppies show no such teat preference and will suckle at any available teat they encounter.

It is very difficult for a dog breeder not to think anthropomorphically, for the dog has been domesticated so long that it has entered into the very fibre of human social structure. Yet there is some evidence that human beings may manifest an innate response to canine needs. A newly purchased puppy left alone at night bleats pitifully, and such is the nature of the cry emitted by the whelp that a human being becomes distressed at hearing the puppy and seeks to comfort it. A few years ago I had an opportunity to test my anthropomorphic views when I whelped a white German shepherd dog in her kennels and brought her to the warm kitchen to rear her litter. Alas, at that time my kennels harboured a particularly lethal strain of *E. coli* bacteria which attacked and caused the death of newly born puppies which came in contact with the floors and whelping boxes within my kennels. But yet litters born in the house which suckled the bitch's colostrum achieved a degree of immunity and could be returned to the kennels within a week of parturition and showed not the slightest sign of *E. coli* infection. Alas this particular litter was born under a heat lamp in the kennels during the night and were several hours old before I discovered them and brought them into the house. Sadly they were infected with the *E. coli* bacterium. They were doomed to die and emitted a curious bleat quite distinct from the cry of a normal healthy puppy. I have bred dogs since childhood and hence was aware that matters were not right, but I was amazed at the reaction of visitors who arrived at my home that Christmas. Friends who were perhaps not exactly antipathetic to dogs, but certainly not dog-lovers, became visibly distressed at the bleats of the ailing and dying puppies – which incidentally all died, despite injections of terramycin, an antibiotic to which this *E. coli* bacterium was apparently susceptible. My views on dog behaviour are, however, regarded as slightly anthropomorphic by those who have conducted their experiments under laboratory conditions.

Might I advance yet another anthropomorphic notion at this stage and suggest that sometimes bitches instinctively realise that a puppy will not survive to adulthood and reject the whelp in the nest, refusing (or not encouraging) it to suckle? Once more perhaps a tale will illustrate a point. During the early days of the development of the breed of terrier I keep, I was plagued by a high incidence of cleft palated puppies in the inbred litters I was producing. A cleft palated puppy has literally no roof to its mouth and cannot suckle, so is doomed to die from the outset. I found bitches rejecting these puppies and pushing them to the side of the whelping boxes, thereby accelerating the death process. At first I believed that dogs, which are as hedonistic as any organism, needed to experience pleasure from the suckling action of the whelps to allow the puppies to continue to suckle, and because the suckling action of a cleft palated puppy afforded the bitch no such pleasure, the dam rejected the whelp. It was a clear-cut explanation that solved the problem neatly – if a shade too neatly perhaps.

However, long after I had solved the problem of cleft palated puppies by judicious line breeding to males which did not carry the disorder, I had cause to doubt my explanation, and question as to whether bitches possessed some innate ability to detect a puppy that was defective and, in true Darwinian fashion, was not affording the whelp the opportunity to survive.

One of my brood bitches – I called her Pagan – whelped and produced six puppies, one of which she promptly ignored and refused to suckle. When I held the puppy to the teat and allowed it to suckle Pagan became quite upset and after six days the puppy looked scarcely larger than it had at birth. I examined the roof of the puppy's mouth, found it to be normal but, despite the fact that the puppy seemed determined to stay alive, Pagan continued to reject it. Returning from school each day my first job was to hold the puppy to one of Pagan's teats to allow it to suckle, but gradually I began to reconcile myself to the fate of the ailing puppy and to my shame perhaps I became less attentive to its welfare!

However on the sixth day after its birth a friend of mine, Terry Ahern, arrived and offered to hand rear the whelp, which was at this stage looking terribly undernourished. Now, despite the fact that the puppy had ingested some of its share of colostrum, and had a certain degree of immunity to canine ills, rearing a whelp from six days of age is no mean feat. It involves not only feeding the puppy a bitch's milk substitute, but cleaning the puppy constantly, not only to remove faecal matter and traces of urine, but to massage the abdomen of the whelp to encourage its bowel movements. If one wishes to rear such a puppy it requires total dedication and there are few with greater dedication than Terry Ahern and his wife Jenny.

The puppy doubled in weight in six more days – no great weight gain for the puppy had been emaciated when Terry had undertaken to rear it – but by the age of five weeks was the same size as the litter mate which had remained with the dam. However, as the puppy grew older it began to manifest a hideous spinal deformity which gave the puppy a hyena-like appearance. I had not detected the deformity and neither had a veterinary surgeon friend who regularly visited my home. Could it be that Pagan had the ability to detect that the whelp was likely to manifest these deformities on the day following the birth of the litter and had decided to cull out the puppy by denying it the right to feed? Truly, the more I know the more I realise how little I know!

Some bitches are particularly slatternly about cleaning their puppies and hence the whelps will soil the litter of their whelping boxes. Most bitches are, however, fastidiously clean about the hygiene of their litters and ingest the faecal matter passed by the whelps. Bitches regularly clean the anal regions of puppies, not so much to remove the faeces but to stimulate defecation. This apparently disgusting habit is of course purposeful and is tailored to keep the wild dog's subterranean nest free of faecal matter which might attract disease. Lairs of wolves are kept meticulously clean, though fox earths sometimes contain traces of faecal matter passed by older cubs.

The fact that puppies, kittens and all the mustelids (the stoat family) are born blind and deaf, while most herbivores are born sighted and able to run at birth is often bewildering to those who are not conversant with animal behaviour. Francis Pitt, the astute Shropshire naturalist, believed that predators are born blind and deaf to restrict their movement until they are old enough to cope with a hostile world. Wild predator kits and cubs are usually very precocious and experience a high cull rate in the weeks immediately after leaving their lairs for the first time. No doubt the cull rate would have been even higher if the kits or cubs were not restricted to the nest until they were old enough to be able to fend for themselves outside the lair. Stoats, weasels and particularly polecats are blind and helpless for quite lengthy periods of time after they are born, and fisher kits are the size of rabbits before they open their eyes.

At ten to fourteen days of age most puppies will open their eyes, thereby heralding in what Scott and Fuller refer to as the Transitional Period of puppy development. To imagine that as soon as a puppy opens its eyes it is able to see, to focus or to receive and interpret visual stimuli would be incorrect. Yet from fourteen days of age a puppy develops rapidly and begins to take an interest in its environment. At this age a puppy will start to notice the presence of its litter mates – hitherto it may only have been drawn to them by their body warmth (puppies often sleep huddled together when the temperature of the whelping box becomes a shade less than ideal).

The transitional period of development is the age when the puppy starts to experiment and develops skills which may be of use in later life. Tyro dog breeders may be astounded to hear puppies of this age attempt a strangled bark, and be even more surprised to find that the puppy too seems astonished at the sound it has created. Likewise puppies of this age attempt to stand and experiment at crawling backwards and forwards. They seek to investigate the presence of certain objects in the whelping box. They may view the presence of the bitch's tail with some interest and mouth interesting objects.

At this stage of the puppy's development, breeders who are not *au fait* with canine behaviour may be horrified to observe the bitch regurgitating food in the corner of the whelping box and the puppies attempting to feed on the vomit. This habit is often made all the more offensive because of the dreadful stench of the regurgitated food, for the contents of the stomach have been bombarded by various digestive juices such as rennin, pepsin and a fairly strong solution of hydrochloric acid before being voided. However this is perfectly normal behaviour and the puppies find the strong smelling vomit exciting.

Wild canines will often catch prey or find carrion, ingesting the meat in large quantities to carry home to the cubs, and cubs and puppies alike can induce the dam to vomit the contents of her stomach by simply nuzzling the bitch's mouth. Most wild dogs carry home partly digested food to their young and the habit has been observed in wolves, jackals, dingoes, Cape hunting dogs and in some species of foxes. The dam's stomach is of course the most convenient carrier available and wolves will often regurgitate as much as ten pounds of partly digested meat to feed a litter.

The unappealing stench of partly digested meat is, however, attractive to the puppies. The food is easily ingested by the puppies and much of the protein of the meat has been partly converted to more easily digested peptones. Furthermore, the vomit has been warmed to body temperature and hence puppies find this food more acceptable and the mess makes a type of food that is readily eaten by a young puppy. Not all bitches regurgitate their food for puppies, though few of the more primitive breeds (malamutes, huskies and Greenland Eskimo dogs) fail to feed puppies in this manner. Curiously some male dogs, even dominant masculine males, can be persuaded to regurgitate the contents of the stomach to puppies. Walden, the alpha male member of my kennels, can often be persuaded to void the contents of his stomach to newly weaned puppies who will nuzzle his muzzle to provoke this reaction. The food is seldom re-eaten by the animal which regurgitates it and it is often wise for the breeder who is whelping the bitch indoors to determine when the puppies have fed and then dispose of the surplus chunks of meat.

Yet the trainer can turn this tendency for a bitch to vomit and the puppies to be attracted to the bitch's face to his advantage with the preliminary training of puppies. Trainers have observed that a whelp which refuses to come to hand when called will readily return to the handler when he drops to a crouch. A variety of reasons were advanced to explain this peculiarity. Some believe that the figure of a person towering over the whelp intimidates the puppy and deters it from coming to hand, whereas the figure of a crouched person gives the puppy greater confidence. Others believe that the sight of a crouched person intrigues the puppy and it comes to investigate what the devil the handler is doing. There might be some substance in these notions, though I am tempted to disregard the theory that the dog is sometimes frightened by the sight of a man walking upright. I served my apprenticeship with a rural springer spaniel trainer who had avant-garde views on dog handling. When a puppy showed a disregard for the commands of the handler my mentor would crouch and begin playing with some stones, muttering inanely as he did so. I have yet to see a puppy which could resist coming to hand to investigate the spectacle.

However, the most logical explanation for why a whelp will come to hand when a handler drops to his or her knees is the fact that the puppy is brought into proximity with the face (and particularly the mouth) of the handler. The sight of the mouth revives racial memories of the dam bringing home a stomach laden with meat which the bitch then vomits to feed her young. It will be noticed that a puppy returning to the handler who has crouched invariably attempts to nose the handler's mouth.

Further proof of the latter theory can be seen when a very young child enters a house in which there is a young dog. The dog will invariably ignore the adults accompanying the child but become quite excited at the sight of the infant. It can be argued that the child's face, being in closer proximity to the dog, rekindles these race memories and this theory is given greater force by the fact that most young dogs will attempt to nuzzle a baby's mouth. Every aspect of dog behaviour should, if possible, be observed and implemented to affect the training of the dog.

Before starting to describe the development of the puppy during the socialisation period of the puppy's development – a brief but so important period of time, lasting perhaps seven or so weeks – perhaps it is expedient to mention something of the importance of socialising any creature. Readers reared on a diet of Mowgli stories (Kipling's *Jungle Book*) or Edgar Rice Boroughs' *Tarzan* would be blissfully unaware of the importance of socialising any creature. Both fictional super heroes are removed from their natural parents at an early age and reared in the company of beasts – Mowgli with a wolf pack and Tarzan with a clan of anthropoid apes. Both develop into marvels of perspicacity with the moral qualities one associated with a well-bred gentleman and the amazing senses of a brute beast. Both characters later accept the civilising influences of society only to detect unacceptable flaws in the characters of their fellow men, flaws which are absent in their animal foster parents. Indeed, neither Kipling nor Rice Boroughs was able to reject Rousseau's notion of the spiritual superiority of the noble savage, though there is considerable evidence to suggest that Kipling may well have had some knowledge of children who had been supposedly reared by wild beasts in the manner of Kamala and Amala, the wolf-children of Godamuri. Kipling's father, John Lockwood Kipling, certainly heard of such tales when he was researching for his comprehensive book *Beast and Man in India* (1891).

However, accounts of wild boys, children reared in isolation either by animals or left to their own devices by accident or design, were commonly repeated in Europe. Linnaeus did in fact classify such children under a distinct heading *Homo ferus* or wild men.

However, the most famous *Homo ferus* was certainly Kasper Hauser, a boy of roughly sixteen years of age who was found wandering in the market place of Nuremburg on 2 November 1828 and whose mind was apparently blank and whose behaviour was that of a very young child. After some tuition he was taught to communicate and was able to give an account of his strange upbringing. He was apparently reared in a hole by 'a man' (Hauser continued to refer to his keeper as simply 'a man' until his death in 1833) who had taught him to stand and walk before bringing him to the market place and abandoning him. Hauser apparently displayed some aptitude to learn but lapsed into moral decline in 1830 and was forgotten, or was treated as one of the curiosities by certain European noble houses at that time.

The psychologist Hebb was fascinated by Hauser and considered that the unfortunate boy's lack of contact with human beings during the formative period of his development was responsible for his inability to adjust to human society. He labelled the results of the socialising programme to which human beings are normally subjected as the 'K Factor' (K for Kasper).

Let us now return to the socialisation period of the development of the puppy, but also keep in mind the peculiarities of tales of *Homo ferus* type children described by Linnaeus – and I make no apologies for the lengthy digression which has brought me to this point in the book.

Although the three week old puppy spends much of its time asleep, this is a period of rapid social development. Puppies allowed to develop in almost feral conditions – I have mentioned tales of farm collies allowed to rear puppies under brushwood – will behave similarly to wild dogs at this stage of their development and will begin to leave the nest to defecate and urinate, declining to soil the bedding in the nesting area. This is the age when owners of wild nesting bitches will begin to notice the presence of puppies, though many of these puppies will display a shyness of human beings and will vanish into their lairs when they are approached. This is also the age when these feral puppies must be caught up and socialised if they are ever to be socialised enough to be trained. If left in their lairs without human contact they will become nervous, intractable and difficult to handle.

During this period of socialising the puppy begins to establish relationships with other members of the litter and develop an elaborate series of facial expressions and tail wagging gestures. Primitive types of dog – the dingo, the basenji ('the barkless dog of the Congo') are apparently somewhat slower in developing the tail wagging gesture than breeds which have undergone a more lengthy period of domestication.

Dunbar describes the tail wagging gesture as performing the same social function as the human smile and this gesture is performed when puppies encounter a familiar litter mate, the dam and eventually the human owner.

Play fighting starts at this age and puppies will pull at the ears, tail and facial skin of litter mates, and sometimes cause considerable pain by doing so, but only by experiment will puppies learn just how hard to bite in play, and learn something of the restraint that is so important in the development of the canine pack structure. Puppies at this stage of their development seem to have little innate knowledge of the warning behaviour of older dogs and it is at this stage that a whelp must learn how to distinguish a hostile situation, or sometimes perish in the process of doing so.

Some bitches, and sight hound bitches seem particularly bad, will attack their own puppies when three week old whelps attempt to feed at the same dish as the dams, though most bitches give ample warning of their intentions long before they snap at a puppy. A bitch may at first attempt to cover the food with her face and head, staring hard at the puppy as she does so. Should the puppy be undeterred by this gesture, she may growl menacingly, and should the whelp fail to interpret this latter warning the bitch may snap at the puppy.

Greyhound bitches, or bitches with strong traces of greyhound blood in their ancestry (lurchers and long-dogs for instance), will often punish a puppy of this age savagely should the youngster fail to heed the warnings she has given it. It is in fact not uncommon to find that a greyhound bitch may bite her puppies so hard that she will kill them, should the youngsters disregard the warnings she gives them as they approach her food, yet she may continue to regurgitate her food and encourage the puppies to eat. My present long-dog is one of these puppies which survived when a greyhound bitch, the mother of eight puppies, became particularly protective of her food bowl.

Once a puppy is three weeks of age breeders usually watch the interaction of puppies and bitch carefully and, should the bitch show a hostility to the whelps at feeding time, feed the litter and the dam separately to prevent damage to puppies. It is by no means uncommon for tyro breeders to report that a strong healthy puppy of three weeks of age has been found dead in its nest box and the cause of the whelp's death is usually that the bitch, seeking to guard its food, has snapped at the puppy. There is indeed some evidence to suggest that the interpretation of canine learning behaviour is to some extent an acquired rather than an innate disposition, though puppies of this age may feign appeasement gestures should a dam growl menacingly at them.

At this point it is perhaps expedient to debunk some of the myths that have plagued dog breeding for hundreds of years. At one time breeders sometimes allowed the bitch to select the puppy the breeder intended to keep. Puppies of three weeks of age were placed some feet from the whelping box and allowed to chill slightly, thereby attracting the attention of the bitch by their plaintive bleating. The breeder then watched to see which was the first puppy the bitch attempted to return to the warmth of the whelping box and kept back this puppy to train. The bitch was supposedly credited with the ability to determine which of her whelps was the most suitable to perpetuate the family. Hence the pointer bitch was able to select which of her litter would be steady at point, the terrier dam which of her puppies would be a fine worker to fox and the collie bitch the most suitable herding dog. Of course this is absolute nonsense which no thinking person could consider to be feasible. Yet the notion is commonly believed by certain dog breeders of working dogs even today.

At the age of three weeks puppies will usually be able to ingest raw meat readily, though breeders often seek to encourage the whelps to eat by feeding them scraped meat. To prepare this a chunk of meat is scraped with a knife until a slimy mess of blood and macerated flesh is removed from the meat fibre and puppies ingest this readily in preference to the solid chunks of meat which often prove a shade too fibrous for the puppy to swallow.

At three weeks of age the puppies' digestive tracts have developed sufficiently well to allow the whelp to be wormed to rid it of roundworms – unpleasant parasites which at one time caused the death of a great many puppies of three to ten weeks of age. Roundworms infest most canines, wild or domesticated, and while it is possible to reduce an infestation of these parasites it is virtually impossible to completely rid a dog of roundworms. These wire-like parasites cross the placenta from the dam to the foeti when the bitch is roughly seven weeks in whelp (I shall deal with this subject presently) and infect the puppies in the bitch's uterus. By the time the puppy is three weeks of age these parasites are very numerous in the puppy's stomach. If the dam has not been treated for roundworms during her pregnancy a puppy may host as many as thirty-four inch long roundworms by the time it is three weeks of age and these parasites must be removed or their number reduced if the puppy is to grow and thrive.

Much of the general public's hostility to dogs can be attributed to the fact that dogs tend to host these unpleasant parasites, and to the fact that human beings can also become infected with this organism and suffer from an unpleasant disorder called visceral larval migrans. This is a complaint caused when the roundworm larvae seek to migrate through the tissues of the human body, or lodge in certain tissues and lie dormant for years. Reports of children having been blinded by roundworm infestations have been recorded and, what is more disturbing, the soil on which dogs have been allowed to defecate usually contains a huge number of roundworm eggs. Parks in which people walk their dogs and allow them to foul are often havens for these parasites and hence one can understand the public's growing dislike of dogs.

Various substances, known as anthelmintics, have been used to cleanse a dog of some, if not all, its roundworms though at one time the treatment for these parasites was often more dangerous to the puppy than the parasite itself. Some worming remedies do in fact smack of witchcraft and were extremely dangerous to the puppies.

One of the earliest anthelmintics commonly used by dog breeders was chewing tobacco and a cud of this vile substance was thrust down the puppy's throat and the muzzle held to force the wretch to swallow. Within an hour of such treatment the puppy would vomit the contents of its stomach, included in which would be a great number of roundworms. The whelp usually became really ill after this treatment and scoured terribly, passing more roundworms together with blood-stained faeces. Many puppies died after being wormed with chewing tobacco.

Some of the herbal worming remedies were equally toxic. Certain pharmacists specialising in the production of canine medicines produced anthelmintics the active ingredient of which was santonin, a substance made from the plant *Artemisia absinthium*, otherwise known as wormwood. Santonin was quite an effective anthelmintic but was so bitter that puppies given this substance often refused to eat for days after this remedy was given them.

These days cheap, readily taken worm remedies such as piperazine citrate or piperazine hydrate are not only efficacious, but rarely cause a puppy of three weeks of age the slightest discomfort. Unless the bitch is kept away from the puppies while this anthelmintic is taking effect no worms will be found passed in the whelping box, for the dam will normally choose to eat the puppies' stools as they are passed and bitches which ingest these stools will usually pass undigested roundworms in their own faeces. Nevertheless, it is wise for the breeder not to allow small children to handle puppies until they have been cleansed of roundworms.

Let us now return to the subject of socialising the puppy. It is possible to wean and rear a puppy from three weeks of age – though I believe it is probably contravening the all-embracing 1911 Protection of Animals Act to deliberately separate a puppy from its dam at this age. However, while it is quite easy to rear litters of this age by hand (a spate of milk fever outbreaks in 1971 caused me to learn how to rear prematurely weaned puppies), if a puppy is separated from its own kind at this age and reared in isolation it will often behave strangely in later life. Time for yet another tale, I'm afraid. Darwin noted that during his five year spell aboard HMS Beagle he visited Patagonia and observed an unusual method of sheepdog training. The Patagonian shepherds – and at that time the country boasted the highest population of sheep in the world – took male shepherd dogs similar in type to white Catalan sheepdogs and weaned them at three weeks of age, keeping them isolated from their own kind and allowing them to suckle milking ewes. The dogs were later castrated and allowed to run with the flocks. Dogs reared in this manner were decidedly hostile to other dogs, disinclined to socialise with them and unhappy when removed from the company of sheep. The dogs were ferocious guards, however, and hostile to any strangers who approached the flocks. It is interesting to note that Darwin made his observations a century before Niko Tinbergen and Konrad Lorenz published their papers on the subject of what Lorenz referred to as *pragnung* or imprinting.

Puppies are sometimes weaned at three weeks of age and reared in isolation in flats and apartments – often denied the companionship of other dogs. The majority of these puppies will grow up asocial or anti-social towards their own kind and appear bewildered when confronted by members of their own species. Most will not only refuse to mate but will appear distressed when another amorous dog or bitch approaches them. Some of these dogs may display a sexual interest in either their owners or in other species such as cats and may become decidedly hostile with owners who attempt to stop the dog's amorous advances. There is in fact a tale of a bull terrier male reared in isolation by its female owner after it had been weaned at three weeks of age that badly mauled its owner's boyfriend when he displayed affection towards the dog's owner. This incident was one of the first accounts of a pit bull terrier behaving strangely and antipathetically to human beings. Usually the breed is surprisingly docile with human beings but this incident heralded a host of complaints which prompted the passing of the 1991 Dangerous Dogs Act.

Yet some dog trainers did (at one time at least) deliberately wean puppies at an early age and rear them in isolation to create a stronger then normal bond between the owner and the dog. The 1830s saw the rise of what Victorian writers wrongly referred to as poachers, who were in point of fact mouchers – petty pilferers of game who were more Autolycus figures (snappers-up of ill-considered trifles) quite distinct from the Fen tiger type of professional poachers who were big-time thieves and quite often extremely dangerous criminals. The moucher simply took game for his own consumption and was usually accompanied on his forays by a hybrid collie/greyhound composite (usually a blue shagg sheepdog/greyhound crossbreed) called a lurcher – large-scale poachers seldom resorted to the use of dogs during their forays. These dogs had an extraordinary reputation for sagacity and Brian Vesey Fitzgerald in *Its My Delight* (1948) considered the lurcher more intelligent than its collie ancestor, but Vesey Fitzgerald perhaps over-estimated the natural intelligence of the beast which was said to be innately suspicious of strangers and which made for home if a person who was hostile to its pilfering owner arrived on the scene.

What Vesey Fitzgerald considered to be natural intelligence was in fact a facet of canine personality conferred by what Lorenz was to call imprinting. It was customary for mouchers to take puppies from their dams as soon as possible and many were weaned at two and a half weeks of age simply because their breeders considered the rearing of whelps to eight weeks or so of age too expensive to consider. The lifestyle of these mouchers branded them as social pariahs and most of them were so antisocial that they discouraged human company. Their lurchers seldom encountered other dogs during the critical socialising period and hence became remote and distant with all but their owners. They were suspicious in the company of any stranger, not just with policemen gamekeepers as Vesey Fitzgerald believed, and when disturbed during a foray set off for the safety of home, sometimes carrying with them their 'swag', for dogs of this breeding often have a natural inclination to 'carry'. Lurchers of this type were not any more sagacious or naturally intelligent than other breeds of dog, but their unique upbringing made them appear so to the uninitiated observer. When their owners died, so imprinted were the dogs and so dependant were they on the company of their owners, that they were often savagely hostile to those who tried to catch them up to rescue them, and the majority of lurchers outliving their moucher owners defied retraining. The history of the famous Greyfriars Bobby would perhaps be equally interesting for a student of canine behaviour to explore.

Once puppies are wormed it is good policy for the breeder to handle the puppies regularly, though care must be taken never to isolate puppies from their litter mates for lengthy periods of time, for reasons already explained. Sensible breeders go to some effort to ensure puppies are properly socialised before being sold and, while Dunbar in *Dog Behaviour* states that it is sometimes possible to repair damage done by undersocialising young puppies, it is wise to prevent them becoming remote rather than taking measures to correct the problems caused by undersocialising. Another tale illustrates this point.

In the early 1980s a new virus caused havoc amongst young puppies and the number of puppies which died as a result of parvo virus was legion. At that time there was no vaccine to prevent the disease and, while veterinary surgeons used cat vaccines to arrest the progress of the infection (the feline infectious enteritis virus is very similar to the microbe which causes parvo virus), this vaccine was far from satisfactory in controlling the spread of parvo virus.

Many puppies contracted the virus just prior to weaning – a time when the antibodies acquired via the colostrum (the first milk secreted by the dam) had begun to wane. Many breeders panicked and went to incredible measures to control the spread of the disease and to protect vulnerable puppies. A few breeders installed closed circuit television cameras in their kennels and potential buyers were allowed to see puppies without touching them, so to speak, and puppies were given as little contact with human beings as possible in their antiseptic surroundings.

The results were unpleasant, though predictable, for the majority of these whelps grew up to be remote and recalcitrant animals which also had little immunity to the sundry disorders to which the majority of dogs are heir, but which usually cause little harm to a healthy dog. The 'dog papers' made much copy of the antiseptic conditions under which these puppies were reared and the emotional damage these conditions caused, which heightened the despondency of breeders who had lost puppies as a result of parvo virus. Fortunately, just at the stage where many dog breeders were considering ceasing breeding, a vaccine which curbed the spread of parvo virus was perfected.

The subject of when it is best to separate a puppy from its litter mates has been debated for quite a long period of time by dog breeders and behaviourists alike. David Hancock of Sutton Coldfield, the world's largest breeder of lurchers, and possibly the world's largest breeder of dogs of any kind, comments that when he sells puppies at eight weeks of age (it is possibly illegal to sell whelps at a younger age) and the buyer returns with the puppy a month or so later, proudly displaying his whelp, there is a noticeable different between the size of the whelp and its now larger and more robust litter mates which have remained at the kennels in Sutton Coldfield. Hancock concludes that perhaps the best time to sell a puppy would be when the whelp is older than the eight weeks advised by most cynologists. Hancock's thinking is somewhat flawed, however. David has made a study of animal nutrition over perhaps thirty years and has perfected a thirty percent protein mixture in order to rear his puppies. This diet, rather than the emotional shock of weaning at eight weeks of age, is the reason for the superiority of kennel reared puppies over their siblings sold off at two months old.

There is in fact ample evidence to suggest that puppies should be weaned at eight weeks of age. At that time puppies are mature enough not to need to suckle regularly – though it is interesting to note that when quite mature whelps are hurt they will often seek to suckle their dams, sometimes quite frantically. (This fact is offered up by those who are antipathetic to tail docking, for it is argued by those in favour of tail docking that newly docked puppies will suckle their dams eagerly.) At eight weeks of age puppies also start becoming hostile to others in the litter and this may well indicate that it is time to separate puppies – and I shall deal with this hostility presently.

An interesting experiment was conducted by the psychologist Michael Fox and the results of this experiment may well indicate the correct age for weaning a puppy. Fox 'wired up' litters of puppies so that they might be given a mild electric shock when they approached the experimenter. Five week old puppies so shocked and left for a week before retesting ran instantly to the experimenter, undeterred by the experiences of the previous week. Twelve week old puppies ran even more quickly to the experimenter when shocked, as if they believed that the experimenter could stop the unpleasant sensation! Not so eight week old puppies, however, which when subjected to the same treatment refused to approach the experimenter the following week.

It is possible to interpret Fox's findings and indeed to put them to practical use by suggesting that preliminary puppy training by aversion techniques – house training and so on – might best be conducted when a whelp is eight weeks of age, and there is clear evidence that a puppy subjected to proper house-training techniques when it is eight weeks of age can be rendered clean in less than a week.

Dunbar in *Dog Behaviour* mentions that most bitches have ceased to suckle young puppies by the time the whelps are seven weeks of age, though heavily lactating bitches, those which have reared two or so litters, may continue to produce milk for a further three weeks. What is more important, however, is Dunbar's observations that after puppies are seven weeks of age the bitch will actively seek to leave her whelps for a lengthy period of time, despite the fact that when the same puppies were five weeks of age the bitch could scarcely bear to be separated from them.

It is interesting to note that breeders often construct a shelf in their kennels, if bitches are permanently kennelled with their whelps after the whelps are seven or so weeks old. Bitches with puppies older than seven weeks usually seek a secluded spot in order to get away from their whelps and sometimes become irritated by the constant harassment of the litter. Some bitches will in fact savage puppies which continue to pester them and breeders construct the shelf or ledge to allow a kennelled bitch to escape her litter for a while.

From the time the puppies are seven weeks of age tyro breeders may be dismayed to find savage fights erupting in the nest box. Some months ago I received a letter from a very upset lady who had bred a litter of standard poodles, which on reaching the age of seven weeks began to battle furiously. Now, contrary to popular opinion, poodles are very sporting dogs with a finely developed hunting instinct. Furthermore, some are extremely game and capable of holding their own in a tussle. Yet the constant battling in the nest box had clearly distressed the lady and I'm sure that my reply that such behaviour was perfectly normal and would abate, and even cease in time, did little to relieve her distress.

It is astounding to watch very tiny puppies of even the toy breed dogs battle in such deadly earnest, and even more astounding to note the trifling events that trigger such furious fights. Desperate battles are set off by insignificant gestures and immediately prior to such battles puppies will attempt to intimidate their potential opponent by walking stiff-leggedly around their foe, nudging the other puppy with a shoulder to provoke some reaction from their litter mate, or mates, for sometimes puppy fights are lengthy and constant and each puppy may fight a dozen or so battles in a single day. Usually the damage inflicted in such fights is minimal and tiny punctures or slashes around the face and ears are all that result from some of the most desperate of puppy battles. Why such furious fights occur at such a young age is the subject of some debate, but it seems likely that battles which test the level of dominance in a litter are best conducted when the puppies have insufficient biting power to incapacitate each other, rather than after the litter has developed permanent teeth and greater strength of jaw. Readers must disregard the to-the-death pack struggles described by Jack London and other writers who knew little of the social behaviour of a canine pack. Animals that are severely damaged during struggles for pack dominance are incapable of pulling their weight in the combined effort to secure food, hence pecking order is usually established either by displays of strength, which are seldom followed by physical aggression, or by puppy battles where superiority is established without great physical hurt to either combatant.

Should a litter not be divided and puppies sent to different homes, a distinct pecking order will have evolved before the puppies develop their second teeth, and this order will have been decided by physical combat. Dog puppies will fight bitches to establish dominance and the fights, while they are often lengthy and testing, will seldom be bloody unless three or more whelps engage in a battle. Dunbar believes that once these fights start to increase in frequency and the durations of the battles lengthen litters should be separated into groups of three puppies. Dunbar is wrong! Perhaps groups of puppies from fairly placid breeds may exist fairly amicably in threes, but it is unwise to kennel more than two terriers, or breeds of a more forceful disposition, together. Indeed, breeders should remember the old hunt service adage concerning the kennelling of terriers, 'kennel three, bury one'.

It is fascinating to watch the play behaviour of puppies of this age, and perhaps such play tells us much of the behaviour of the ancestors of the domesticated dog and how little domestication has buffed the behaviour patterns of the modern domesticate. Puppies will start to stalk each other long before leaving the nest, one puppy sometimes apparently deliberately taking on the role of the prey, while the other will act out the part of the predator. Puppies will crawl towards each other in a feline, rather than canine manner, making use of any cover or obstacles to complete the stalk before pouncing on the whelp which is acting out the part of the prey. Those who are not *au fait* with the behaviour of certain types of hunting dog may be surprised to watch this cat-like stalking technique but adult sight-hounds allowed sufficient liberty to develop a style of hunting will attempt to catch quarry in this manner. A greyhound sighting a hare feeding perhaps a quarter of a mile distant will attempt to walk up to its quarry, rather than simply exploding into flight after the creature in the style required of a coursing greyhound. The hound will walk towards the hare almost on tippy-toe, and freeze when the hare stops feeding and raises its head to observe the hound. Once the hare resumes feeding the hound will continue to stalk its prey until it is close enough to possibly catch the creature in fair flight.

Groos believe all play is preparatory – it prepares the animal for its role in life and facilitates its future survival. It is all the more remarkable that puppies of seemingly effete lap dogs, which apparently have no heritage of hunting, will as puppies manifest the self-same stalking ability as the most predatory sight-hound puppy. The reader must remember that, despite the fact that the dog has been domesticated for perhaps twenty or so thousand years, it still retains many of the qualities of its wolf-like ancestors. Like a Golding child hero, this animal is able to slough off the veneer conferred on it by a civilised life-style and revert to the behaviour of one of its primitive ancestors. It never fails to horrify and amaze pet keepers that the most innocent of lap dogs, allowed to run at liberty, will sometimes wreak havoc on sheep and other livestock. The dog, no matter what the breed, no matter what the upbringing of the animal, is essentially a hunter and needs little encouragement to exploit its hunting instincts.

By the age of eight weeks, long before a social hierarchy of the litter has been established, puppies will have developed distinct discernable personalities. At eight weeks of age dominant, ebullient puppies will be observed in the litters, as will quiet, retiring whelps which will often be crowded out at the food bowl. At six weeks of age many bitches will be larger and apparently more dominant than male puppies of the same age, though by eight weeks male puppies are often more confident and forthcoming than their sisters.

Tyrannical whelps, puppies which are furiously dominant, so dominant that they terrorise other puppies at feeding time, may be evident in a litter, and sometimes these puppies are smaller than some of their litter mates, though a puppy which dominates the food bowl at feeding times will usually outgrow its subordinate litter mates unless it is removed from the nest box or whelping kennels while the others feed.

Some eight week old whelps can be very overbearing with their litter siblings. I once bred a litter of white German shepherd dogs puppies which were a very level type and well socialised but in their seventh week one male, a medium-sized yellow coated animal, began to terrorise the other whelps, snarling furiously if one of the litter approached the food bowl and furiously attacking any litter mate that attempted to feed. He displayed no animosity while I handled him as he fed and was very sycophantic and submissive with human beings, even at feeding times when some whelps may seek to warn human beings who touch them. As time went on it became expedient to separate him at feeding time, whereupon he became furiously protective of the empty feeding tray.

There is some evidence to suggest that breeders would do well to select puppies to suit certain clients or guide the purchaser's choice of whelp. I would be very reluctant to place a very dominant, ebullient puppy with a shy, retiring, nervous person and would never allow a harsh, obviously heavy-handed person to claim a quiet, slight nervous whelp. Constant ownership of a dog or dogs often allows a person to be able to assess his own personality and determine which puppies in a litter might suit him or her. My own personality defects – I am not particularly sociable, fairly easily upset by criticism and not very outgoing – dictates that I seldom choose male puppies to train and normally select quiet bitches with sunny dispositions. I fare quite badly with dominant males which sometimes need a heavy hand to discipline, but I usually make a very good job of training less dominant bitches of the same breeding.

The mismatching of an owner with a puppy is often a recipe for disaster, particularly as many people are reluctant to accept their own character weaknesses. Desperate problems arise when a socially inadequate person seeks to own a breed of dog that is bred to be dominant and aggressive, simply as a prop to his own character weakness. A showing of the film *The Omen* usually sets the phones ringing in kennels specialising in the breeding of huge Rottweilers, for the film depicts the breed as a furious guard of the demon child Damien Thorne. Likewise, the film *The Boys from Brazil* produces a spate of clients eager to buy large Dobermann males.

Certain breeds of dog that have been bred to be aggressive towards human beings – Dobermanns, Rottweilers and some strains of German shepherd dog – need careful handling and breeders would do well to advise unsuitable would-be owners of the danger of buying such breeds. Social inadequates are often reluctant to purchase smaller, less dominant bitches and usually seek out large and very dominant dog puppies. The result of this mismatching of furiously dominant male dogs with less than dominant human males was made manifest by the spate of attacks perpetrated by Rottweilers in 1989, and it should be noted that virtually every attack was made by a male rather than a bitch Rottweiler. I shall deal with the subject of matching dog with owner at a later stage in this book.

Yet the reputation achieved by the pitbull terrier which led to the passing of the Dangerous Dogs Act of 1991 is hard to explain. While a pitbull terrier puppy may well display a dominance over other puppies of other breeds, the breed had an admirable reputation for being steady with even small children, and a name for being tolerant with people. Ed Reid, who was responsible for bringing the breed to Britain, comments that the breed achieved poor results in the Shutzhund tests in Germany simply because with most pitbull terriers it is difficult to generate enough antipathy to human beings to encourage the breed to attack, though once the pitbull terrier has learned to take the fight to a human being the damage the beast can inflict is often devastating. Reid attributes the spate of man-biters reported in the breed prior to the passing of the Dangerous Dogs Act of 1991 to the fact that breeders have simply bred from undesirable, untypical stock.

Adult dogs often show a great tolerance of puppies and will often allow the youngsters to take great liberties with them. Puppies can often be seen clambering over mature males, exploring the adult's nose, eyes and of course its mouth, without incurring the wrath of the adult. Yet the same adult male often reacts with great fury at the sight of another sexually mature dog. Male wolves display similar restraint when pestered by young cubs and allow considerable familiarity without retaliation.

Even when puppies overstep the mark and cause a mature dog to retaliate in some way, puppies are seldom damaged by even a grouchy, bad tempered male dog. My own alpha male, a huge white German shepherd dog, is very tolerant of puppies and allows them to swarm over him, to pull his fur and to insert their heads between his cavernous jaws – a habit in which most small puppies tend to engage, possible as a memory of the time when the pressing of a head into the bitch's mouth caused her to regurgitate the contents of her stomach. He may lift his lip in a snarl, an action that seems to cause the puppies to turn their heads away from him, presenting their sides and flanks to him. His growls, deep-throated and ominous enough to deter all but the most persistent human visitors, seldom produce a reaction from tiny puppies, though a few may manifest placatory gestures such as lifting a forepaw and touching the older dog's face and turning their heads away from Walden.

Lorenz describes the classic puppy placatory gestures in his book *Man Meets Dog*, when a tiny dwarf pincher of eight weeks of age met a giant Newfoundland male. The tiny puppy was terrified at first and rolled on his back ejecting a tiny stream of urine as it did so, as if to say 'I am a puppy, I pose no threat to you. Please do not hurt me'. Yet not all dogs are tolerant of puppies and a dog owner with a recently acquired puppy would do well to observe the relationship between a puppy and an adult dog before leaving the pair alone. A tale illustrates the point. I write a weekly column for a magazine called *Countryman's Weekly* and receive many letters from dog owners with problems. My role of canine agony aunt is an interesting one: in October 1991 I received a letter which illustrates the dangers of leaving a puppy alone with a hostile adult dog. A young couple with a fairly sunny, fell-type terrier of three years of age purchased a lurcher puppy and introduced the pair to each other in the late afternoon of the day they acquired the puppy. The puppy, newly weaned and denied the company of its litter mates, sought out the older dog and behaved in the typically sycophantic manner one might expect of a newly weaned puppy. The older dog failed to respond in the manner suggested by Lorenz and sought to clamber onto window ledges and furniture to escape the attentions of the whelp, which incidentally seemed bewildered at the behaviour of the older animal.

It is amazing that the couple, after observing the antipathy of the adult dog to the young puppy, decided to leave the pair unattended for the night. As a seasoned dog keeper might expect, the older dog, driven to desperation by the puppy, killed the youngster during the night. To expect the rigid social behaviour reported by Lorenz is to court disaster. Some adult dogs kill puppies with alacrity, heedless of the 'I am a puppy. I pose no threat to you. Please do not hurt me' gestures manifested by a whelp. Similarly some puppies never seem to learn the meaning of the hostile gestures displayed by older dogs.

In passing, and rather out of context, Lorenz mentions that few dogs will attack or hurt a bitch, despite the fact that a mature female dog may behave in a very churlish manner with male dogs. Yet bitch dog fights are not unknown and are rather common amongst the breeds which have been specifically bred to be aggressive. Pitbull terriers are often quite hostile to bitches of the same breed which do not display a readiness to mate, and owners of working terriers often report instance of dogs which have set upon and killed adult terrier bitches.

Some eight to twelve weeks after the puppy has suckled the antibody with the first milk or colostrum the whelp will have lost much of the immunity conferred by the maternal antibodies and is open to infection from the five major ills which beset dogdom – distemper, hepatitis, leptospiral jaundice, parvo virus and canciola fever – and should be inoculated against these infections to give the puppy the vital protection it needs.

The optimum time for this inoculation is of interest to the dog keeper for a puppy inoculated before it has lost the maternal immunity conferred by its dam will possess antibodies which will negate the effect of the inoculation, or render it useless. Similarly a puppy left until these antibodies have dwindled to a very low level is in great danger from the diseases previously mentioned.

In America, where pet owners seem to be more fastidious about the welfare of their animals, it is a common practice to have a puppy blood-tested to ascertain the exact level of antibodies in the bloodstream before inoculating the whelp. If the puppy still has a high level of maternal antibodies, the veterinary surgeon will advise the owner to wait a while before inoculating the whelp. If the antibody level is low the puppy is inoculated immediately.

In Britain it is customary to simply make an appointment to inoculate the puppy when the whelp is eight weeks of age, though many breeders inoculate puppies to protect them against parvo virus some weeks earlier than this, and at this point perhaps it is expedient to describe the five major illnesses that can beset a dog and the measures one can adopt to protect the animal against them.

Prior to the perfection of canine vaccination programmes, distemper was the bane of young dogs and killed a large number of animals before they reached maturity. One of my hobbies is to collect advertisements for livestock and during the 1920s the appraisal 'over distemper' was an important evaluation of a young dog's worth.

Distemper was a constant worry for the commercial kennel owner and the pet keeper alike. Will Humpheries, the world famous setter breeder, once told of three kennels which went bankrupt when distemper invaded the premises and how two owners committed suicide and the third took up holy orders. A variety of quack medicines which claimed to protect puppies from the ravages of the disease were advertised in the 1920s and 1930s, including the much vaunted nostrum Lucanis, supposedly perfected by Sir Jocelyn Lucas, the famous Sealyham terrier breeder. All these potions had one thing in common – they had absolutely no effect on the progress of the disease and neither did they prevent the appearance of the infection.

The disease is caused by a group of viruses rather than by a specific microbe and each virus produces slightly different symptoms in the infected dog. In 1948 Laidlaw and Dunkin divided the distemper complex viruses into three divisions, labelling them A, B and C. Virus A was a very virulent type of virus which invariably killed or disabled dogs it infected. B was a very uncommon type of virus which manifested a variety of symptoms, while virus C was a commonly encountered virus which gave rise to only mild distemper symptoms from which most dogs recovered.

Puppies infected with any of the distemper viruses usually suffer far more than adult dogs infected with the same virus. Infected dogs become feverish, develop gasto-enteritis like symptoms, lung disorders and the characteristic dry nose and pus filled eyes described in early Victorian dog books as 'distemper warning signs'. A particularly virulent type of distemper known as hardpad (once called para distemper) appeared in 1948 and caused the pads of the feet to harden to such an extent that the infected dog clattered when it walked.

Treatment of an uninoculated dog is usually far from successful. If a dog is kept warm, given antibiotics to stem the onset of various diseases introduced by the weakening effects of distemper (antibiotics have no effect on the distemper virus itself) and given electrolyte solutions to drink to compensate for the dehydration incurred as a result of scouring, then the dog may recover only to manifest symptoms of fitting, chorea and paralysis. However, it is unnecessary to know how to treat an infected puppy, for by inoculating against this disease the dog keeper can protect the animal against the horrors of distemper. Current thoughts suggest that if puppies are inoculated against the disease at nine weeks of age they should be given a further inoculation at twelve weeks, by which time maternal immunity will be negligible.

Veterinary surgeons advise a further booster inoculation when the dog is two years of age.

Leptospiral jaundice is an equally dangerous and distressing disease that can also be avoided simply by inoculating the dog against this ailment. This disease is also important because it can be transmitted from dog to man and is then referred to as Weil's disease. The infection was once referred to as 'rat catcher's yellows' and a great many vermin catchers who caught live rats to supply the infamous rat pits (which became illegal in 1911 – 1912 in Scotland) died from this infection. Monlux, in a survey conducted in America, showed that 55% of all healthy rats carried the disease, but long before Monlux conducted his research into the disease dog breeders were advised to keep kennels free of rats. Certain kennels mentioned by both Trapman and Lucas were so heavily infested with rats that it was impossible to rear puppies to more than ten weeks of age, for it is assumed that the maternal antibodies conferred via the colostrum waned before that period and the puppies died of leptospirosis. What is even more disturbing is the fact that should a dog be lucky enough to survive the infection – and the majority of dogs do not, one must add – the animal continues to excrete the leptospiral jaundice spirochaete in its urine for up to eighteen months after the infection. Hence even when kennels were cleared of rats it was often still impossible to rear puppies on the premises. Furthermore, kennel staff were in constant risk when working alongside infected dogs or dogs still passing the spirochaete in their urine. Few manual labourers are totally free of cuts and abrasions sustained during their daily work and the spirochaete finds little difficulty entering these wounds and infecting the worker. In 1981 seventy-two cases of Weil's disease were reported among farm workers and others who had contact with the infection, and seven of those infected died.

A dog infected with the organism will suffer from loss of appetite, severe dehydration and a yellowing of the skin and whites of the eyes – hence the name 'rat catcher's yellows' – and kidney failure usually follows hot on the trail of such symptoms.

Ratters or those who bred and trained rat-killing terriers to compete in the infamous rat pits were wont to wash out the mouths of their dogs with peppermint water, made by boiling peppermint leaves in water and adding a dash of gin to the cooled liquid. This was said to prevent the yellows and also to clean out the wounds inflicted by rats on the dogs' gums and tongue. Of course this nostrum failed to work, penicillin and expert veterinary help is more efficacious, but inoculation of the whelp is the only answer to the disease, for not only is prevention far better than cure where leptospirosis is concerned, but it is far cheaper, for an infected dog needs constant and lengthy treatment if it is to recover from this infection.

Hepatitis or inflammation of the liver is another dangerous disease that can be prevented but seldom treated. Old veterinary books suggest that an infected dog may appear perfectly well the night before and dead the morning after, so rapid is the progress of this disease, but many dogs may live long enough to display obvious symptoms of the infection. Infected animals may vomit copiously, scour so badly that the faeces are stained with blood, and display a characteristic blueing of the eyes – a condition known as keratitis.

Dogs which apparently recover will harbour the disease for months and the virus which causes the illness will survive on the kennel floors and walls for many weeks. Most of the canine marking points of towns and cities – lamp posts, trees, fire hydrants – were at one time rich sources of hepatitis infection.

This is a ghastly disease which is extremely difficult and costly to treat but it is easily prevented by a vaccination programme, and frankly it is lunacy to buy a puppy, spend a great deal of money on its rearing, but neglect to inoculate the animal against the deadly ills described. It is wise not to exercise a whelp in places where it might encounter other dogs, or the body wastes of other dogs, until it has been inoculated and to wait two or so weeks after the vaccination programme to allow the whelp to develop a level of immunity before taking the youngster to places where it might encounter other dogs. Uninoculated dogs are sources of infection and the distemper outbreak of 1993 which caused the death of several puppies was credited to an infected uninoculated dog left behind by travellers.

The juvenile period of puppy development begins when the whelp is roughly ten weeks of age and lasts until puberty (Scott and Fuller suggest puberty begins at six months of age) and is the time when whelps explore their environment and attempt to establish relationships with their owners and with other dogs. It is also the age when wild canines experience a heavy cull rate as a result of the youngsters' explorations. A high mortality occurs amongst fox cubs of this age and many become victims of motor vehicle accidents. Others are killed by dogs, for many cubs of this age will show little fear of venturing onto territory where hostile dogs may be present.

Dunbar mentions an experiment where puppies were raised in a one acre paddock. The puppies so raised stayed close to the nest box and seldom roamed twenty feet from the kennel until they were twelve weeks of age, whereupon they began to explore the rest of the field: wolves also have little inclination to wander far from the den until they are three or so months old.

Hunting dogs of all breeds show little of their instinctive hunting ability until they are at least twelve weeks of age and many will only display an interest in quarry species when they are nearer the end of the juvenile period of development when they may suddenly develop an interest in hunting certain prey. This transitional period of development is often very rapid and one day the whelp will show no interest in hunting while the following day it may galvanise into action at the sight and scent of quarry. This precocious behaviour often gives the tyro handler a false impression of the ability of the youngster. Inexperienced handlers often tend to pressure a youngster of this age into the work required of an adult dog. Trainers of retrieving breeds will often sicken a puppy of this age by encouraging the whelp to repeatedly fetch objects long after the youngster has tired of the game. Owners of sight hounds are often amazed at the speed with which a puppy develops an interest in chasing when it approaches six months of age and make the mistake of allowing the whelp to chase hares – the most taxing of quarry for a sight hound.

Terrier puppies often display a great deal of aggression towards quarry at this age, but this aggression is not reinforced by the maturity that it necessary before the handler enters the puppy. Tyro terrier men have ruined a great many young terriers when they misinterpret this youthful aggression and allow the young dog to be overmatched by entering it to foxes. The precocious behaviour of puppies approaching maturity may give the trainer a false impression of the animal's maturity, and it is wise to remember the whelp is still only a very immature animal at this age. It is interesting to note that hunting, and for that matter herding, dogs begin to display some propensity for the work for which they are bred at roughly the same age as wolves and wild dogs start to make an active contribution to the welfare of the pack. It appears that the lengthy period of domestication that has produced the dog has dulled few of its instincts.

Dunbar makes a pertinent point concerning the start of the juvenile period of canine development – ten weeks of age – namely that the dog's learning capacities are fully developed by the time the whelp is ten weeks of age and that henceforth it becomes increasingly more difficult and time-consuming to train a dog. To explain Dunbar's premise more succinctly and more simply, it is amazing just how much an experienced trainer can teach a ten week old puppy in a very short period of time. Even Middle Eastern sight hound puppies can be taught to retrieve, to come to hand and perform rudimentary obedience work if taken in hand at eight weeks of age or slightly older, but it becomes very difficult to obedience train these hounds if they are allowed to go untrained until they are perhaps a year or so old. Dunbar explains this by the statement that new learning is often dissident with established behaviour patterns in an older dog. Yet this is only partly the truth. If an animal is taught by using play methods – certainly the best and easiest way to train a puppy – a young puppy is more inclined to enter into the game than an older dog and hence is more easily trained. Providing the trainer is aware of the limited attention span of the whelp and the puppy's desire to learn by playing, a puppy can be rendered virtually half trained by the time it is twelve weeks of age, though the trainer must be aware of the whelp's relatively poor mental coordination and must adapt his training programme accordingly.

For instance, while very young puppies will willingly clamber over objects to get to their owners (and this is the beginning of training a dog to jump) it is unwise to encourage a mite to attempt to clamber up great heights, not simply because the whelp may be strained or hurt attempting this jump, but also because it has not sufficient co-ordination to effect a landing. Likewise very young puppies usually show a great enthusiasm for retrieving attractive objects, but to repeatedly throw an object and encourage a puppy to fetch that object will often sour a puppy so badly that it may refuse to retrieve in later life. It is indeed a monumental task to retrain a dog to retrieve once it has sickened of the activity. It is in fact so easy to ruin a willing young puppy simply by considering that because of its precocious behaviour it is a mature dog. Puppies are so often overmatched, over trained and prematurely entered by newcomers to dog training.

Dunbar makes an interesting point concerning the different ways puberty effects dogs as opposed to bitches. A bitch that is sexually immature may behave as if terrified when an adult male approaches her and adopts a posture indicating a courtship display. The male may approach her with its tail raised and wagging, its face displaying no hostility, yet a young bitch may squeal with terror and attempt to escape the dog's attentions, tail tucked between her legs and the fur along the spine raised in fear. Yet the male has no hostile intentions to the female.

A few days before a bitch approaches 'heat' she may play with the same male in a coquettish manner but snap at him should he become too amorous. Days before she may have appeared terrified of the same male and may have raced off and hidden to escape his attentions.

Male dogs start to display a sexual interest in bitches when they are as young as four months and may attempt to mount members of their own litter at this age. Young males will in fact mount other males as eagerly as they will females of the same age, but to interpret such behaviour as being in any way perverted is ludicrous. Dogs of this age are exploring their own sexuality and the sexuality of other dogs. Likewise young males of this age will display the leg lifting gesture when urinating, though most will continue to urinate at a crouch in the same manner as a bitch.

It is highly unlikely that puppies of this age will succeed in mating a bitch, and even more unlikely that they will be able to fertilise her, though puppies of six and seven months of age are often fertile and quite virile. A puppy of six months run on with his dam will often, if allowed, mate with his mother when she comes into season and succeed in putting her in whelp. At one time outrageous notions concerning canine versions of the Oedipus complex were advanced by behaviourists to explain how easily such an incestuous union might be effected. These notions were absurd, though a dog kennelled with its dam will not only be able to sexually experiment with her as puberty approaches but will be more confident with her than he would be with a strange bitch. The majority of breeders are able to tell tales of unexpected incestuously bred litters that have resulted from young dogs serving their dams, though a young male will usually make many unsuccessful attempts at mating before he succeeds in effecting a union with any bitch. Young males of the smaller breeds such as toy dogs, or some of the smaller terriers, are particularly precocious with their own dams, while the giant breeds of dogs such as Newfoundlands, Danes and either of the wolfhounds (Irish and Russian) are rather slower in maturing and the males are often quite infantile until they are a year old. It is also interesting to note that females of the giant breeds are equally slow in become sexually mature and may not come into season until they are two or three years of age.

The slow sexual maturation of greyhounds has been mentioned by many authors. Hancock of Sutton Coldfield, who probably has the world's largest kennels of breeding greyhounds, believes that as in-season greyhounds are not allowed to race or course, an unintentional breeding programme has produced bitches which are late in coming into season and only stand for mating once a year. Yet once these bitches are mated they will come into heat twice a year as will normal dogs. Whether or not hormone injections which allow a bitch to be raced and coursed more regularly by retarding her natural seasons have altered the breeding cycle of certain bitches is hotly debated by breeders who make use of 'cast' greyhound breeders to produce lurchers.

Thus the stages of canine development from birth to puberty – the canine ages of learning perhaps, for this is the time when the dog will be more receptive to train than at any time in its life. It is of course, to abuse a cliché, possible to teach an old dog new tricks, indeed police and security services regularly recruit the services of mature dogs to train, though usually not dogs of more than two and a half years, one must add. However, it is far easier to teach a puppy the basic rudiments of obedience. Victorian dog books usually advise the would-be trainer to leave the dog untrained until it was six months of age before considering it for training, but there seems to be little logic behind this notion. Vesey Fitzgerald, though scarcely an authority on the training of dogs, believed that so great was the Victorian dog trainer's fear of distemper that dogs were often left in kennels until they were considered to have some immunity to this disease. However, modern vaccines now offer virtually one hundred percent immunity and hence it is absurd to allow a dog to remain untrained until it has outgrown the most receptive period of its life.

The Adult Dog

I am not exactly antipathetic to the words of wisdom supposedly uttered by Victorian dog keepers, though much of the advice offered by the spate of dog training books written in the 1850s must be considered as utter drivel. However, there is an element of truth in Trapman's statement that 'a dog grows upwards in its first year, outward in its second and matures in its third year'.

Many small or toy dogs are almost fully grown by the time they are six months of age, though in 1976 the recently formed Jack Russell Terrier Club of Great Britain decreed that a terrier could only be considered as fully grown when it was eighteen months of age – the debate was triggered by a dispute about the sizes of the two types of Jack Russell terrier and eventually led to the formation of the breakaway Parson Jack Russell Terrier Club. Yet few dogs are physically mature at a year old and are certainly not mentally mature at this age. Greyhounds raced or coursed hard at this age often become physically damaged, sustaining injury to lungs, heart and diaphragm, while eighteen-month-old hounds subjected to the same treatment are seldom injured in the same way.

Many male puppies are born with their testicles fully descended and the rest usually have their testicles descended before the whelps are six months of age. At this stage perhaps it is expedient to explain the difference between monorchidism and cryptorchidism as many dog books hopelessly muddle the meanings of these terms.

True monorchids are rare and have only one testicle – and are not animals that have one descended testicle and one testicle concealed in the dog's abdominal cavity. This condition makes absolutely no difference to the dog's ability to reproduce its own kind but usually prevents a dog from being shown, or at least winning under Kennel Club rules. There is in fact a tale which illustrates, if nothing else, the measures to which certain breeders will go to win a coveted rosette (value 10p). A certain exhibitor owned a monorchid and the dog was an excellent specimen of the breed. However, such are Kennel Club rules that the presence of only one testicle barred the animal from being shown, let alone winning, at a show. Some months later the exhibitor appeared in the ring with the same dog which sported two testicles. Now it is possible for a unilateral cryptorchid (I shall explain the term presently) to 'drop' the other testicle if given hormonal injections, so other exhibitors rather grudgingly accepted the dog's win. Later, however, it was suggested that the animal was indeed a genuine monorchid and that the exhibitor had persuaded a veterinary surgeon to insert a plastic testicle into the dog's scrotum – such is the desire some people have to win, one supposes.

Most dogs with one obvious testicle have the other gonad anchored in the intestinal cavity and are referred to as unilateral cryptorchids. These dogs are also able to reproduce their own kind and are not in any way less vigorous than normal, entire male dogs. Hormonal injections can sometimes induce the other testicle to descend into the scrotum. Should these hormonal injections fail to produce the desired results, the undescended testicle may cause the dog some discomfort and may become cancerous. Hence many veterinary surgeons advise that an undescended testicle which has failed to respond to hormonal treatment be removed surgically to prevent complications in later life. The operation to remove an undescended testicle is relatively simple but should never be attempted by a layman.

While dealing with the subject of cryptorchidism it should be mentioned that a bilateral cryptorchid, a dog with neither testicles descended, may display normal sexual behaviour but is unlikely to be able to breed, though many are highly sexed and will attempt to mount and mate a bitch. What causes this physical peculiarity is debatable but Geoffrey West in *Blacks Veterinary Dictionary* suggests that while it is an inherited condition, rats fed a biotin deficient diet were found after two or three weeks to have their testicles withdrawing from their scrotums and embedding in their intestinal cavities.

The current trend of emasculating any male dog that is not required for breeding is in some ways commendable, for it does reduce the incidence of unwanted litters resulting from wandering male dogs serving equally wayward in-season bitches. Indeed one seldom sees the spate of miscellaneous street curs one saw shortly after the end of World War II. Wandering male dogs with amorous intentions can be a great nuisance and the cause of not only a number of traffic accidents but also canine attacks on human beings, though most males seeking a mate are seldom hostile to passers-by who deliberately ignore the dogs.

However, I feel I may well have run ahead of the theme of this chapter and perhaps it is necessary to explain why certain owners seek to castrate their dogs, and the methods employed to remove the dog's gonads.

Dunbar (*Veterinary Review*, 1975) suggests that while the majority of people seeking to have their pets castrated do so in order to prevent the animals from breeding, some request the operation in order to reduce or ameliorate the dog's undesirable characteristics such as aggressive behaviour, mounting sundry animate and inanimate objects and spraying and marking objects in the owner's house.

Dunbar suggest that there appears to be no obvious reduction in these undesirable characteristics after castration. Indeed, many dogs may even continue to copulate for several months after gelding. Many males continue to manifest aggression towards other dogs and some continue to spray furniture and even the legs of human visitors to the house. Cats, however, once castrated, will virtually cease spraying (and this is a particularly unpleasant habit amongst tom cats) within a fortnight after castration.

Many dog keepers who have had their wards castrated after the dog's habit of spraying has made the house uninhabitable say that, while the castrates may continue to spray after being neutered, the strength of the urine passed by the castrate is less offensive than the urine passed by the male when it was entire. A local dog breeder always advises purchasers to castrate their males for this reason. It would therefore appear that once a dog has manifested undesirable characteristics of the type described, castration will not ameliorate its behaviour. However, there is some, albeit slight, evidence to suggest that an animal castrated during puppyhood may not manifest aggressive tendencies towards its own species. Malamute sled dogs are fiercely aggressive towards other sled dogs, though the bitches are less aggressive, and 'mushers' were wont to castrate males as puppies to reduce the incidence of fights between sled dogs. It would therefore seem that castration might prevent displays of aggression in males, but will not curb aggression once the problem has manifested itself.

It would appear that the owner should think long and hard about emasculating a male dog, for the castration process is obviously irreversible. Clearly, a dog which may contribute good qualities to the gene pool of a particular breed, or maybe a member of an endangered breed, should only be castrated as a last measure. Indeed, it would be difficult to find reasons to justify the castration of such an animal.

Yet castration of the dog is a reasonably simple operation if conducted by a qualified veterinary surgeon under sterile conditions, though the operation should never be conducted by anyone unqualified to perform such surgery. Under sterile conditions and with the correct instruments haemorrhage is rare, hernia very uncommon and peritonitis (the plague of the unqualified castrator) virtually non-existent, though if peritonitis does occur it frequently causes the death of the animal.

Entire sexually mature males often behave strangely when nearby bitches come into season. Many well-trained, obedient dogs become remote and unresponsive to commands when an in-season bitch is in the vicinity of the home training area or kennels. Some will refuse to eat, lose weight rapidly and behave in the manner of a Shakespearean lovesick swain. Retrieving breeds may decide to retrieve intermittently, and drug detecting dogs behave less than efficiently when their thoughts are distracted by the scent of in-season bitches.

This lovesick attitude has been often used to the advantage of those who are determined to outwit guard dogs being used to protect certain properties. Rags soaked in the vaginal fluid of in-season bitches (shades of Rabelais) retain their scent for months if kept in refrigerated conditions and these can be cast into compounds to distract the attentions of guard dogs. Better still, an in-season bitch held outside the enclosure in which free running guard dogs are kept (as opposed to dogs accompanied by human handlers) is efficacious in attracting the attentions of male guard dogs of any breed.

When dog thieving and the ransoming of stolen dogs was a lucrative business in Victorian Britain, in-season bitches of any breed found a ready market with professional dog thieves. These thieves would wait for several hours with an in-season bitch on a leash, until the dog these thieves intended to capture was turned out of doors to perform its bodily functions. These dogs were then enticed away by the in-season bitch and held for ransom. Elizabeth Barratt Browing's dog, Flush, which had escaped an unpleasant fate at the hands of her fearsome father, probably fell victim to the charms of an in-season bitch and was ransomed for £50 – an enormous sum that represented a year's salary for a schoolteacher at the time.

I cannot resist an anecdote related to me by a trainer of sniffer dogs – dogs trained to detect the presence of narcotics and sometimes explosives. A consignment of marijuana was being brought into the country and, for those who are not *au fait* with the nature of *cannabis indicus*, the drug is so strongly scented that a human being can detect the presence of a large quantity of the plant. Drug dogs are trained to go wild with excitement when quantities of these substances are secreted in hiding places, for they regard the search as an exciting game – hence the drug is usually enclosed in sealed airtight bags in an attempt to evade the attentions of sniffer dogs. One consignment of this drug was brought into the country aboard a ship that carried an in-season bitch and quantities of rags soaked in the vaginal fluid of the bitch were concealed in areas far distant from the consignment of drugs, to attract the attention of the sniffer dogs away from the marijuana. Luck, however, did not favour the drug smugglers for the usual sniffer dog, a springer spaniel male (and springers often make the finest of sniffer dogs) had been laid up by some accident and a crossbred bitch had been brought in to replace the dog. She displayed slight interest in the scented rags for a moment or so, before totally disregarding the scent and promptly seeking out the haul of drugs. Tales of these remarkable dogs are seldom related but are well worth the telling, though it is likely that the handlers are required to sign Official Secrets Act documents to prevent these tales becoming public. It is a pity if this is the case, for the tales of the sagacity of these dogs, many of which are gentle gundog breeds which display not the slightest animosity to the smugglers, would constitute the material for an excellent book.

The task of the dog warden or dog catcher is a particularly odious one, especially as many of the dogs caught by them finish up in what is euphemistically known as a 'dog shelter' – a decided misnomer for many of the inmates enjoy only a brief spell of captivity before being destroyed. Yet in estates where dogs are allowed to run the streets an in-season bitch becomes a nuisance to end all nuisances. Dogs congregate in great numbers outside the homes where the bitches are kept and will sometimes perform amazing feats to get into houses and mate with these bitches. Large, powerful dogs have been known to bite through doors to mate a bitch, and in one instance a small dog clambered onto the roof of a run-down bungalow and became stuck in the chimney as it attempted to descend to mate with an in-season bitch.

Dogs in waiting, so to speak, will lie around the homes of in heat bitches in a listless manner and seldom attempt to fight each other for the right to mate bitches and it is these packs of lovesick dogs that have become such a nuisance on certain estates. Usually some social order of dominance has been developed at a very early stage in the development of the pack and a show of superiority, rather than a hostile confrontation, has decided this pecking order. Usually a stiff-legged, strutting ritual will cause one of the would-be antagonists to back down and assume a subservient role in the pack structure.

Yet there is some indication that these lovesick males are far from the semi-dormant, docile beasts they seem to be and, when a pack is attracted to an in-season bitch, certain members of that pack can be hostile to human beings who approach them. By the age of twelve I had a considerable knowledge of the behaviour of such packs, for I was employed as a part-time delivery boy by the local grocers and I learned to identify hostile alpha males amongst the packs of dogs which gathered outside houses of local in-season bitches. Many were indifferent to my approach, but some of the more powerful dominant males often displayed aggression as I approached the house which held the bitch. When I succeeded in making my delivery, and facing down the hostile males in order to do so, the aggressive males immediately went through a marking ritual, spraying plants, posts and corners of walls immediately I left the house to which I was delivering groceries.

Postmen, the most common victims of canine aggression, often report that an in-season bitch attracts a host of hostile male dogs, though it can be argued that many of these males may have been equally hostile if placed in conditions where their behaviour had not been triggered by the presence of in-season bitches. However, visitors to houses where dogs are waiting to serve an in-season bitch would do well to beware hostile males within the group, for the sight of a dog attacking any creature, man or beast, is terribly infectious and the excitement engendered by the attack can often induce even the most subservient dog to join in the battle. In passing, it is worth noting the behaviour of males which are watching other males copulate with bitches. Despite the fact that certain males display a furious antipathy towards each other, I have yet to observe a male attack another male that is mating a bitch or has succeeded in tying with the said bitch. Males may display a bristling antipathy to the successful suitor, tied with the bitch and in a very vulnerable position during this 'tie', but I have yet to see even a very hostile male attack another that is so engaged in mating. Certain codes of conduct are rigidly observed by wild and domesticated canines.

Most dogs are intensely polyerotic and a dominant male left to roam free will mate a great number of bitches. Lorenz in *Man Meets Dog* is, however, a little sceptical about the polyerotic nature of chow chows and related breeds of dog and his scepticism is seemingly shared by Terrasse, who made a somewhat more exact study of the behaviour of this remote oriental breed of dog. Lorenz, who incidentally believes the chow chow is an example of a lupine breed of dog (a dog descended from wolves, whereas he considers German shepherd dogs to be descended from jackals), believes the chow chow to be monogamous. He quotes the instance of a bitch chow chow who refused the attentions of a succession of males which Lorenz considered desirable to use for breeding, only to mate with a male of her choosing.

If the reader will forgive a slight digression, chow chows may well be a distinct species of canine only slightly related to other breeds of dog. Terrasse records the urine/blood count to be different from that of ordinary domesticated dogs – and quite different from other spitz types which closely resemble chow chows. Terrasse also mentions that when subjected to strain or injury the chow chow's bones fracture in a distinctive manner. It is interesting to note that when allowed to run at liberty, chow chows seem almost reluctant to enter into the pack structure enjoyed by other dogs, and most other breeds either shun or are actively hostile to chow chows. Yet chow chows will of course mate with both wild and domesticated canines and produce fertile hybrids. Indeed, Lorenz suggests that an attractive and possibly useful new breed could be created by mating chow chows to rough collies, though perhaps it would be a little difficult to find a use for such a hybrid.

Yet Lorenz's deductions are not perhaps as logical as one might expect from a scientist of his calibre. Breeders often report that when an in-season bitch 'displays' to a male in her kennels and is considered ready for mating, the breeder may wish to seek the services of a dog some miles distant and may take the bitch to the said male. When introduced to the new male the bitch may not be prepared to stand for the dog. Indeed, she may behave in a very hostile manner towards him – and some of my stud dogs have been badly bitten by visiting bitches. When the bitch returns home she once again behaves in an amorous manner to a male from her own kennels. It can be argued that the journey to a distant kennel will unsettle a bitch, but the return journey to her own kennels after an unsuccessful attempt at mating her is obviously as long, yet some bitches will then immediately stand for a male of their choosing.

Lucas was of the opinion that should a bitch refuse to stand for any dog other than a male of her choosing she should be allowed to mate with that dog, regardless of her breeding (providing he was of the same breed, of course) and the quality of the stock he had previously sired. Lucas did in fact believe that some almost divine force compelled the bitch to seek out a particular mate and couple with him. He quotes an instance when a particularly fine Irish setter was produced when a great field trial champion bitch refused to mate with a fine male the breeder had selected, but became extremely attracted to a poor Irish setter male the breeder had decided to 'draught' – to sell to a less than discerning buyer. The union of the top grade bitch and the down market male produced one of the best litters of the day. Lucas certainly had unusual ideas about dog breeding and failed to see that the bitch was probably one of those rare treasures – a prepotent female – who will produce top grade puppies when mated to virtually any male of the same breed. I cannot resist finishing with a tale related to me by this truly great raconteur, for it further illustrates my point. The dog, once it had coupled with the bitch, was sold for a song to a nearby farmer who tethered the creature and used it as a guard dog (some setters and pointers make extraordinarily good guard dogs if restricted by a chain). When the litter bred by this male had proven its worth in the field, the owner of the bitch sought out the services of the draughted stud dog and was charged ten times the sale price of the male as a stud fee, and the fee increased as litter after litter produced champions and high grade workers. The owner of the stud, flushed with the breeding success of the wretched chained-up guard dog, offered the animal at public stud, but the dog never once produced even second grade animals when mated to over a score of top grade bitches. Lucas told me this tale a decade before his death but failed to accept my explanation that the brood bitch was simply a prepotent dam and that the initial mating had not been engineered by some divine force.

Some dogs are in fact attracted to bitches which are, to human beings at least, particularly unsavoury looking creatures, and the reason for this attraction is quite easily explained. Unkempt looking bitches with locks of matted hair, as have my own strain of working bearded collie, are often irresistible to dogs which will travel a great distance to court such an animal, yet ignore the immaculately groomed in-season bitches in the next street. A bitch that is, to use a term, sanitised, rendered deodorised enough to be tolerated in a human dwelling, is probably not heavily scented enough to attract an assortment of male dogs. A rather unpleasant analogy may well illustrate just how important the olfactory sense is to the attention of the opposite sex: Napoleon once wrote to Josephine, 'I shall be home in two weeks – don't wash'!

My most matted coated bearded collie, a bitch which defies grooming and whose locks seem permanently matted is particularly alluring to all my stud dogs and to assume that the cartoons which indicate that particularly masculine-looking bulldogs are lovesick at the sight of well groomed, ribbon bedecked French poodles is decidedly anthropomorphic. If I might cast in yet another tale to illustrate a point which shows how certain species are sexually excited by scents and sights which are repellant to others, may I mention the odd behaviour of domesticated ducks. My own runner drakes are particularly excited by the sight of a duck that is muddied with the filth that is part and parcel of every well-used duck run and, once a duck is so mud bespattered, other drakes will attempt to mate her so often that she will be literally drowned by the attentions of her amorous suitors. Hence it is wise to move a duck that is being so abused by drakes to save her life.

There is obviously a reason why I relate these tales of the sexual behaviour of birds and beasts for by the study of these peculiarities breeders and keepers of dogs can learn much. It is customary for a bitch that is about to be taken to a stud dog to be washed and groomed by her owner, possibly to create a good impression on the owner of the stud dog. The arrival of a well groomed, deodorised, sanitised bitch may certainly impress the owner of the stud but the stud dog may be less excited by the well washed, well presented bitch. Young males which have not served bitches may in fact be deterred by a bitch whose pheromonal scents have been reduced or masked by washing and grooming and curiously most bitches are equally attracted by the scents of strongly scented male dogs. Some bitches may shun the attentions of males that are in pristine condition yet become wildly excited by scruffy street curs which are so strongly scented as to be objectionable to human owners.

I have deliberately mentioned that during the process of mating a dog with the bitch the bitch should be taken to the dog and not the dog transported to the premises with which the bitch is familiar. A stud dog is happier if allowed to serve a bitch on his own territory, a territory he has 'marked' with traces of his own urine. Some studs will boldly mate bitches in the bitch's kennels but others are less willing to copulate under these conditions. A male may often refuse to even engage in a courtship ritual with a bitch when the dog is taken to unfamiliar territory to copulate. Perhaps London's dominant primordial male dog was indeed a figment of the author's imagination!

The marking tendency of mature adult males – males will lift their legs and pass a few drops of urine (usually very pungently smelling urine) on objects – can be fairly distressing to house-proud dog owners, particularly if visitors insist on bringing other males or near season bitches into the house, but such territory marking is a perfectly natural action. A hostile resident male dog that has just engaged a rival male in either a physical skirmish or a facing down ritual – for dominance is not usually decided by physical combat – will often deliberately urinate over furniture and against corners of walls. On a more macabre note, pit dogs which have fought and slain other dogs will deliberately mark the corpse of their dead foes.

Frankly I am extremely chary about allowing visitors to bring their dogs over the threshold of my home, not because I am automatically antipathetic towards other people's dogs, but simply because I am not prepared to accept the antisocial behaviour such visits provoke amongst my own dogs. A visit from someone who not only insists on bringing a dog to my croft, but refrains from leaving the animal in the car and brings it indoors, will immediately cause my own house dog to spray the furniture, and no amount of chastising (or castration for that matter) will prevent the male dogs behaving in this manner. The house dog has not suddenly become 'dirty' – what all embracing terms human beings use to describe the behaviour, both social and sexual, of animals – but it is simply the dog's way of reasserting its 'presence' on the house in which it lives. The arrival of a young puppy of either sex will seldom provoke the same reaction from an adult dog.

Mature males being exercised in places where other dogs abound will often behave in a manner the dog keeper considers peculiar or irrational, and one of the most baffling gestures may be the sight of a dog having sprayed, marked or defecated, vigorously striking its hind legs on the earth with such force as to leave striations in the soil. At one time this action caused some confusion among cynologists, but the force and frequency with which a dog performs this exercise is due to the proximity of in-season bitches which have used this portion of the soil to urinate or defecate. When bitches which are in season or near season use these patches of soil the dog will usually 'scrat' vigorously, but seldom engage in this activity if no bitch has marked the spot.

Males are usually or invariably larger than bitches of the same breed but the reason for this phenomenon, referred to as sexual dimorphism, is difficult to explain. It has been argued that amongst wild canine packs smaller, less powerful pack members are often required to drive the prey towards the larger, more powerful pack members who are required to dispatch the prey, but this is simply not the case where packs of domesticated dogs are concerned, for bitches, and sometimes very small bitches, may well display a greater propensity for killing the prey than the more powerful males. Amongst wild canines such as wolves the hunting strategy often seems to be determined by the older females rather than by males, though this peculiarity is easily explained. Wolf packs, or indeed packs of other wild dogs such as dholes, are usually led by older females, or rather a particular hunting technique seems to be determined by them. This does not imply that female canines are more intelligent than males but rather that packs are usually simply extended families of dogs – grandmother, mother, children and so on – which have learned to reply on the hunting technique of the oldest pack member. Tales of desperate leadership battles belong only in the fiction written by Kipling and London!

Many zoologists and behaviourists have attempted to explain the phenomenon of sexual dimorphism and it would be unwise to leave the subject without at least a passing reference to what is known as the Moors Erlinge hypothesis, and I beg the reader's indulgence for the following digression that is necessary to explain the theories advanced by these zoologists.

In few species is sexual dimorphism more evident than among the mustelids, a family that embraces stoats, weasels, ferrets, polecats, otters, badgers, fisher martins and sables. Male ferrets are almost twice the size of females born to the same parents, but amongst fishers the size difference is most noticeable, for male fishers weigh a massive 12 lbs while females scale in at perhaps 4 lbs. Ecologists once believed that this size disparity allowed both sexes to share the same territory, with the smaller females preying on smaller birds and certain animals into whose lairs the females were able to gain entry, while the males were able to pull down and feed on animals which were larger and more powerful.

Now such a theory clearly does not apply to the wild canines which were probably the ancestors of the domesticated dog, though it may be feasible that solitary canines such as foxes could benefit from the difference in size between the sexes. Yet animals which rely on pack hunting techniques to secure food, packs in which both females and males feed on the same prey carcass, would not benefit from the difference in size between males and females of the same pack.

A more sophisticated hypothesis was advanced by Moors and Erlinge who arrived at their conclusions independently after exploring the behaviour patterns of mustelids. Both argue that females are smaller so that they may conserve their energy while carrying and raising a litter. This hypothesis rather comes apart at the seams when one examines the subject of sexual dimorphism amongst predatory birds, for example female falcons and hawks are much larger than the males. Male peregrines are in fact referred to as tiercels, which means they are two thirds the size of the female peregrines.

I will in the tradition of the intellectual coward leave the reader to unravel the mystery surrounding sexual dimorphism amongst domesticated dogs and conclude this chapter with a reference to the fearsome Beasts of Gevaudan which between the years of 1764 and 1767 killed and partly devoured at least sixty-four people. C.H.D. Clarke (1971) is of the opinion that these outsized canines were dog/wolf hybrids not wolves, but when the elderly hunter Antoine de Bauterne killed the beasts the male was found to measure 32 inches at the shoulder and to weigh 130 lbs, larger by far than the biggest European wolf. The female, identically coloured to the male, was a great deal smaller!

The Adult Bitch

Frankly there is little evidence to prove the popular belief that nestling bitch puppies during the socialisation period are any more precocious than the males of the same litter, though many breeders believe this to be the case and defend this notion vigorously. At this stage of the development of the whelp the sexual dimorphism that becomes evident in later life is not apparent and there is little difference in size between the sexes.

Litter fights, nestling battles, call them what you will, are common and bitches and dog puppies will fight each other savagely with no regard to the social codes that are evident when either party reaches sexual maturity. As I write my work is subject to constant disturbance, for a litter of ten-week-old terrier puppies are playing (a delicious euphemism, considering the way the whelps behave) beneath my window and furious battles are being enacted between a powerful young bitch and a like-sized male of the same litter. The battles are ferocious and the pair grapple with the intensity of mature American pit bull terriers fighting each other to a standstill, standing panting and exhausted after each battle, only to resume the conflict when the pair have recovered their breath. In a week or so I shall divide up the litter to prevent damage to the puppies, pairing off the four puppies, for contrary to the notion advanced by Dunbar, the kennelling of three puppies of this age is thwart with danger and will often result in the death of one of the whelps: two puppies will lock in a face to face conflict while the third will work at the soft abdomen of one or both of the antagonists. Terrier fights are often desperately ferocious affairs, but when either dog or bitch puppy reaches sexual maturity a curious pattern of behaviour between the sexes begins to emerge.

Shortly before the onset of sexual maturity many bitch puppies will behave as if terrified by the appearance of an adult male dog. At the end of the juvenile period (10 weeks of age, perhaps) the self same bitch puppy may greet the same adult male as she would her dam, running towards the male eagerly wagging her tail, rolling on her back and attempting to press her muzzle in the proximity of the adult's face, for reasons previously explained. Yet a mere month or so later the same bitch will often feign terror at the approach of the same male, running away, tail tucked between the hind legs and bleating and cowering in terror. Bitch puppies will often display the same behaviour pattern no matter what the breed or size of the male dog they encounter. It is often a ludicrous sight and embarrassing to the tyro dog owner who is not conversant with the behaviour of puppies to see a leggy Great Dane bitch puppy fleeing in terror when confronted by a tiny but mature Yorkshire terrier dog.

Why bitches approaching sexual maturity behave in such a manner often confounds breeders and behaviourists alike. Suggestions offered in doggy periodicals and sporting magazines do not stand up to scientific scrutiny. One theory offered is that while mature males are usually fairly tolerant of sycophantic puppy behaviour they are less tolerant of the same behaviour from older animals. Yet some males are decidedly dangerous with young puppies and one must add some bitches will slaughter other bitches' puppies with great ferocity.

Yet another notion is that young bitches nearing sexual maturity are in danger of being sexually molested by mature males and hence behave in a terrified manner when approached by such a mature male. This too is a ludicrous notion by any standards. While some dogs persist in harassing bitches which show no sign of sexual readiness, the majority will tend to ignore her or pay only a passing interest should the bitch show an indifference to their advances. Few dogs display a satyr-like interest in a bitch that is sexually immature or in a mature bitch which is not ready to receive a dog.

So what therefore is the reason for mentioning the peculiar behaviour of a sexually immature bitch when a mature male approaches her? Training of the bitch (or dog) puppy is best conducted during that period of time described by Scott and Fuller (1962) as the socialisation/juvenile period, a time when a bitch puppy is likely to manifest this panic-stricken hysterical reaction to the appearance of an adult male. Thus when I am training or even exercising a young bitch off the lead in a public place where a male dog might suddenly appear, I am extremely wary for I have observed a terrified bitch puppy 'cut and run' at the mere appearance of a male and disappear for several hours. When I am exercising a young bitch who is running free, as soon as I observe a dog of any breed and of either sex, I leash up the bitch and keep it leashed until the other dog has disappeared from sight. The reason for the stark terror most young bitches display when confronted with a strange, sexually mature male dog still remains a mystery.

The majority of medium sized bitches will become sexually responsive to the advances of a male dog when they are roughly nine months of age, though some bitches, particularly very tiny toy breeds, may become sexually mature at the age of six months. Larger breeds such as Great Danes, Newfoundlands, Irish wolfhounds and mastiffs may be considerably older before bitches of these breeds are sexually receptive. Similarly, greyhounds may often be of retirement age (4 to 5 years of age for the racing and coursing greyhound – a remarkably short time) before they show the slightest sign of coming into season, but this apparently late sexual maturity amongst greyhounds is not as inexplicable as it may appear. Greyhound bitches are prevented from racing or coursing for a certain period of time before and after a season simply because, not only would the appearance of an in-season bitch distract other male greyhounds (and certain females as well), but a greyhound bitch is said to develop a layer of fatty tissue around her heart when she is in season and the build up of fatty tissue places a tremendous strain on the constitution of an animal that is required to run at speeds in excess of thirty miles an hour. It is possible that by an unintentional process of selection greyhound bitches which are late coming into season have been produced by breeders of competition dogs. If I might elaborate still further to explain this hypothesis, greyhound breeders seldom engage in a complex breeding programme but simply mate the fastest, most consistently successful bitch to an equally fast and consistently successful unrelated dog. Thus a bitch which is regularly in season (and hence is barred from competing immediately before and after her season) would seldom 'notch up' a formidable record of wins. Such a bitch may therefore be less likely to be used as a brood to produce further litters. After a very short period of unintentional selection it is likely that greyhound bitches produced from successful broods may be less frequently in season and may not come into season until they are two or three years of age.

Hancock of Sutton Coldfield has another theory to explain the delayed sexual maturity of greyhound bitches and suggests that trainers resort so often to the use of oestrogens and gonadotrophins to prevent a bitch coming into season and not being able to compete at certain events, that its sexual cycles are thrown out of kilter. This, however, does not explain why some greyhound bitches are slow to reach sexual maturity and may not experience their first season until they are over two years of age. It is worth noting some of Hancock's observations concerning in-season greyhounds, however. Some greyhounds may come into season once a year, others once every two years, but once these bitches have produced a litter the majority will come into season every six months thenceforth.

As a bitch approaches her first (and subsequent) season she will usually manifest an improvement in her general condition. She will usually begin to look more rounded and her coat will usually develop a more lustrous sheen. This will of course be more apparent in smooth coated dogs such as whippets, Dobermanns, Rottweilers and greyhounds than in longer coated breeds such as Afghan hounds, deerhounds, rough collies and Old English sheepdogs. Likewise the internal organs of a bitch nearing season will usually develop fatty deposits, possibly to sustain the bitch should the pregnancy be a lean one. In fact an experienced dog breeder is usually able to determine when a bitch is approaching season simply by observing her general condition, but this improvement in condition is not always apparent in bitches that are approaching season.

Lurcher rescue societies and other groups who are prepared to take in badly fed, sickly and mistreated animals often report that some of the most ill nourished, desperately ill looking bitches will often come into season despite the fact that they are obviously unwell and unfit to breed a litter. Metcalf likens this last ditch attempt to breed to the fact that when groundsel has germinated and developed seed leaves, if the plant is denied water it will produce flowers immediately after the seed leaves in an attempt to perpetuate the species, even at the expense of the mother plant. Quite often lurcher rescue societies are given pregnant lurcher bitches which have been abandoned by travellers and are in a wretched and pitiful condition. Yet these bitches have come into season, accepted the service of a male dog and conceived despite their emaciated condition. In passing it must be added that many of these bitches will abort their litters, despite the care lavished on them by the rescue societies who, incidentally, perform an admirable service to dogdom, but some of the most pitifully thin, starved and ill-kept bitches have been known to produce live, though undersized, puppies.

Very young bitches which come into season at six months of age – or in some exceptional cases even younger – will accept the attentions of males and conceive. However, the most commonly posed question from tyro or first time dog breeders is whether or not it is wise to breed from bitches during their first seasons and whether breeding from an animal at this young age does any harm to the bitch in her later years. The subject of breeding from a first season bitch is such a hotly debated one that I beg the reader's indulgence for the amount of time I shall devote to the subject.

Firstly, the expression 'first season' is a shade loosely defined, for while some bitches may achieve sexual maturity by or before the age of six months, other breeds, particularly the so-called giant breeds, may not come into season until they are four years of age and may be considered fully grown at this age. Thus breeding from a four year old bitch during her first season is not only advisable but good sense if the bitch is to be used as a brood.

Those against breeding from a very young bitch during her first season suggest that the bitch is too physically immature to be a brood and is still in the process of growing. Readers may recall the edict passed by the Jack Russell Terrier Club of Great Britain that a terrier should not be considered fully grown until it is eighteen months of age. Conversely it should be remembered that young girls who produce babies when they are twelve years of age do not appear to be stunted by this early pregnancy.

Few very young bitches, aged nine months or less, appear to be mentally or emotionally mature enough to rear a litter. However, despite the fact that both the pregnancy and the parturition may be normal and seemingly both effortless and painless, some are apparently baffled by the appearance of the whelps, while others may be hostile to puppies who attempt to suckle. Others abandon their litters, ignoring the whelps despite their pitiful bleating. In passing it is worth mentioning that some Siamese cats are also indifferent to their first litters and some early breeders even advised allowing pure-bred young Siamese queens to couple with house cats so that the first litter, which was highly likely to be abandoned, would have little financial value – I shall deal with the myth of telegony later. Perhaps later litters would be lovingly cherished by these queens, despite their indifference to their first mongrel brood. This is also true of very young bitches who would reject their first litters but display strong maternal tendencies towards their second crop of puppies.

There is little doubt that very young bitches do not lactate as heavily as do somewhat older, more mature bitches and my personal observations reveal that a bitch lactates most heavily during the rearing of her second or third litter (an observation based on the fact that at one time my strain of terrier was plagued with milk fever or hypocalcaemia). Hence the young bitch's first litter might not only be ill-cared for, treated with indifference by the dam, but also ill fed as some very young bitches lactate badly when rearing their first litter. I hasten to add that I have also seen very young bitches lactate very heavily.

My own personal feeling about breeding from a bitch during her first season is that a bitch of this age would be better employed in training, growing and playing rather than taking on the duties of motherhood – but such sentiments are decidedly anthropomorphic and based on the fact that my experience with dogs has been largely with animals that have been bred to work or to fulfil a practical function.

There is, however, a school of thought that believes that breeding from a young first season bitch is advisable and sometimes beneficial. This school of thought suggests that a bitch whose pedigree is of the highest calibre should be encouraged to breed as soon as possible to ensure the continuance of the family, for all manner of accidents might befall the bitch and prevent her breeding at a later date. The same school also argues that a first litter might serve as a valuable 'practise run' for the bitch and ensure she is experienced enough to rear her second litter satisfactorily.

It has long been noticed that young animals, and human beings for that matter, usually produce their young with less effort than older animals of the same species. It is believed by some, and I must stress the term 'some', that the pelvic bones of young animals are softer and more pliable than the bones of an older animal and hence are able to bend to allow the passage of a puppy through the birth canal. It is certainly true that older bitches often have more trouble giving birth than do younger animals.

At this point, before returning to the subject of the young bitch approaching her first season, it is perhaps time to debunk a hoary old myth. Veterinary surgeons are frequently asked as to whether it is wise to allow a bitch to breed a single litter for the health of the bitch. It is assumed, rather unscientifically as it happens, that a bitch should be allowed to fulfil her sexual functions just once in her life to remain in good health. Nothing could be further from the truth. Many bitches are prevented from having litters and yet live to a great age, experiencing perfect health until their dotage. Indeed, there is some evidence to suggest that a bitch which is allowed to bear a single litter is in greater danger of contracting metritis and pyometra (inflammation of the womb and pus in the womb) than a bitch which is denied the right to rear a litter, or a bitch which is kept primarily as a brood and allowed to produce many litters.

On the subject of myths I feel I cannot omit to mention the theory of telegony – an absurd notion that was at one time commonly believed. This theory suggests that the first mating influences not just the puppies born from the union, but the whelps born in subsequent litters. Hence, if a pure-bred bitch escaped, was served by a cur and produced a litter she was often given away as she was considered ruined for future breeding, for all her subsequent puppies would be tainted with mongrel blood. This is an absurd notion but one which is still believed by some.

So, having performed my traditional and expected role as an iconoclast and destroyed many popularly held theories, perhaps it is time to return to the subject of the bitch which is approaching her first season. The first hint that a young bitch may be coming into season is manifested by her behaviour and mental attitude, rather than by any physical peculiarities. A young bitch approaching sexual maturity may behave skittishly and display a certain disobedience to commands, whereas hitherto the same animal may have appeared delighted to obey the owner in any way. This apparent disobedience is not due to a deliberate stubbornness on the part of the bitch (in fact the owner may do well to eschew the expression 'stubborn' from his vocabulary where the training of any dog is concerned) but simply due to the bitch's heightened awareness of the scents, sounds and sights of other animals of her own species. She may be called to hand and come readily until she encounters a patch of soil that has been fouled by another dog and then, heedless of entreaties and commands, insist on sniffing the patch of soil, savouring the odours with a quizzical expression on her face as she does so.

During a training session the sound of a dog barking nearby may cause her concentration to break and for her to disregard the training exercise. A week or so previous to this time she may totally ignore the most frantic barking emitted by other dogs and have eyes and ears only for the trainer. As she approaches season she may well find any sound made by another dog little short of irresistible and choose to ignore the trainer's commands.

The appearance of another dog, be it adult or puppy, will produce a similar break in concentration and one must be prepared for the sight of an in-season or near season bitch breaking training to race off and cavort with the other dog, even though a month or so previously she may well have exhibited panic at the sight of the same dog. As she approaches season she may endeavour to chase after the dog heedless of the pleas of the handler and engage the dog in a characteristic play ritual, standing with her stern towards the dog but behaving almost indignantly should the dog endeavour to sniff her genitalia.

Frankly there is little or nothing a handler can do to remedy the situation and there are no panaceas to help the trainer over this rather difficult patch in the bitch's development. I have owned bitches which were rock steady as puppies, allowing horses and cattle to approach them and yet not 'cutting and running' at the approach of these animals. Yet as the bitches approached their first season they behaved irrationally and displayed great disobedience – and frankly I expect such behaviour and compensate or make allowances for it. Yet I repeatedly hear handlers refer to the 'stubborn' behaviour of in-season bitches. Should either a dog or bitch manifest any of the symptoms of appearing 'stubborn' it is simply an indication that the handler is failing to communicate with or failing to understand the emotional state of the animal.

Shortly before the bitch displays a readiness to mate her vulva will begin to enlarge and become turgid. Furthermore, on handling the bitch's hind quarters a swollen, almost tube-like bulge will appear from the vagina to the spot beneath the bitch's anus as the vagina too starts to become turgid and swollen to prepare for penetration by the male. I make a point of handling bitches daily, even when I ran a terrier pack of over sixty terriers, and running my hands along their genitalia to ensure they are not approaching season when they are running with dogs, for nothing creates greater carnage than an in-season or near season bitch running in a mixed pack (a pack composed of both dogs and bitches). It is in fact wise for the pet owner and kennel hand alike to pay particular attention to the physical condition that indicates a near season bitch.

Near season bitches are a great liability in a domesticated pack situation – and it is possible that the monogamous nature of wolves and other wild dogs may well have developed to cope with the effect a near season bitch may have on the rest of the pack. A bitch in this condition may flirt and cavort with every male in the pack (and also with many high ranking dominant females) yet refuse the attentions of the males aroused by her cavorting. The males thus aroused by the behaviour of the bitch may attempt to mount her and may bump against each other while doing so, often precipitating furious battles in which other males and bitches may join, though the bitch whose behaviour has triggered the fight will seldom join in the conflict. For the reasons described handlers of packs of hounds – bassets, beagles, harriers, foxhounds and staghounds (and particularly terrier packs) – are careful to separate near season bitches from males long before these bitches are actually ready to mate.

About this time the bitch may experience an increase in appetite. Some may consume disproportionate quantities of food and this probably accounts for the improvement in condition – some in-season bitches positively glow with health – and for the depositing of fat around certain organs, particularly around the heart, hence the rule excluding in-season greyhounds from track and field events. This increase in appetite is perfectly natural and should cause the dog owner absolutely no concern.

A few days after the swelling of the bitch's vulva becomes obvious to the stock keeper a few drops of blood may be observed seeping from the genitalia and over the next few days the quantity of blood discharged via the vagina will increase greatly. Some bitches are scrupulously 'clean' (a deliciously anthropomorphic expression) about removing the blood from the genitalia and the stock keeper may not notice the animal is bleeding however copious the flow of blood may be. Others may be more remiss about cleaning their sexual organs and leave larger drops of blood wherever they travel – so much blood in fact that first-time dog owners become alarmed at the 'haemorrhage' and in panic call in a veterinary surgeon. This is a totally unnecessary course of action for such bleeding is perfectly normal and part of the bitch's oestral cycle.

Small bitches produce a smaller quantity of blood-stained fluid at this stage but some of the giant breeds lose large quantities of this fluid at this period and at the time when the bitches are losing the greatest quantity of blood they will refuse to stand for mating. Nor will an experienced stud dog – a dog which has served a large number of bitches in the past – pay a great deal of attention to a bitch which is losing a large amount of blood, though most experienced stud dogs will casually sniff the genitalia in much the same manner as they will any bitch, in or out of season, which is brought to their kennels. Only when this copious bleeding has begun to abate and the bitch's vulva has swollen to its largest will the bitch stand for mating and the experienced stud dog attempt to mount her.

This of course poses the question as to why a bitch loses such a quantity of bloody fluid, or more to the point, why do bitches shed this bloody fluid if they are not willing to allow a dog to mate them when they are bleeding most heavily. It has been argued that wild dogs shed little of this fluid prior to standing for mating and the scent of this bloody fluid may serve to prepare the wild canine male for the fact that the bitch is nearly ready to mate. It has also been argued that this shedding of bloody fluid may serve to attract the attention of wandering wild canine males to the presence of an in-season or near season bitch. Yet, if Fiennes and Fiennes are correct in their hypothesis that certain species of wolves are the ancestors of domesticated dogs, it should also be noted that these wolves live a communal though monogamous existence and leave the extended family or pack a few weeks prior to parturition, and hence would not need to produce large quantities of bloody fluid to advertise that they were near to, but not quite ready, to receive the attentions of a male wolf.

It is also worth noting that a domesticated bitch which is shedding blood quite heavily will seldom attract the local dogs in the same manner as will a bitch which has virtually ceased bleeding but is sexually ready to mate with a male dog. Only when the bleeding has virtually ceased will local dogs really make a nuisance of themselves.

An extraordinary explanation of this phenomenon was offered by Thompson in 1962 in a brief, unscientific but cleverly written article. Thompson suggests that this heavy bleeding prior to mating is a process that has evolved since the dog has become domesticated and has evolved to alert the owner of the dog, rather than male dogs, that the bitch is almost ready to receive a male and, if the owner should so decide, he should be ready to take the bitch to a male. Wild canines which bled copiously would attract the unwelcome attention of predators which seek to prey on such canines – wild dogs of all sorts have always been attractive fare for the larger felines, one should add. Now Thompson's theory has its flaws, and obvious flaws at that. It is believed that primitive peoples – the Australian aborigines, the people of New Guinea – did not associate the act of copulation with either pregnancy or parturition and hence it is unlikely that they would consider a near season bitch was indicating that she was desirous of producing puppies.

When a bitch is ready to stand for mating her vulva is swollen to its maximum size and has unfolded in the manner of certain flower buds opening to attract pollinating insects. A bitch in this condition is exciting even to the mature and experienced stud dog and should a male dog attempt to mount a bitch in this condition she will turn her tail aside to assist the union and thrust her vagina towards him to allow the dog to penetrate her, but I shall deal with the subject of mating, pregnancy and parturition presently.

An in-season bitch, a bitch which is ready to receive the attentions of a male dog, can often be the very devil to contain to prevent her mating, often with the most unlikely and unsuitable males. Owners of pit bull terriers – fascinating dogs despite the present legislation concerning them – often report that out of season bitches which have shown a willingness to fight male pit dogs to the death will, when in season, bite through wooden doors to mate with the self-same dogs. One breeder reported that her bitch climbed up a chimney and leaped from the roof of a bungalow to encourage a dog chained in the yard to mate with her.

Paul Sagar, who courses and breeds salukis, is of the opinion that these aloof desert greyhounds often show a marked preference for mating with their own kind and in-season bitches will sometimes spurn the attentions of males of other breeds to mate with salukis. Yet the abundance of saluki-bred long dogs attests that salukis will not always disdain the sexual advances of other breeds of dogs!

Kennel bred bitches will often press their genitalia against the bars of their kennels to encourage male dogs to mate them 'through the bars', an incongruous sight but one I have observed twice. A few years ago I took a bitch to be mated to a dog that lived near London and after mating her to him returned home. That night I awoke to hear a screaming emanating from my kennels and found the bitch tied – through the bars – to the dog kennelled next to her. A mixed litter resulted, but I shall explain this phenomenon presently.

The nuisance caused by an in-season bitch attempting to seek a mate is often too much for many pet keepers and there has been considerable research into the production of oestral suppressants – substances which suppress the tendency for bitches to come into season. The most common one is megestrol acetate, a substance which is a synthetic equivalent of a naturally occurring hormone. Megestrol acetate has been marketed by Glaxo under the brand name Ovarid but such substances should be used not only with care, and only under veterinary supervision. It is also of interest that megestrol acetate is also used to treat forms of feline eczema or dermatitis. Prolonged use of this drug may well produce adverse effects including hypertrophy of the uterus and certain mammary gland problems.

However, the use of megestrol acetate based oestral suppressants is certainly preferable to spaying the animal. Not only are modern oestral suppressants virtually foolproof, but should the owner of the bitch decide to breed from the animal the owner has merely to discontinue the use of the chemical for the bitch to come into season and produce a normal, healthy litter.

Spaying or the surgical removal of the bitch's ovaries is permanent and sterilises the animal henceforth. The operation is a relatively simple one though it is beyond the capabilities of a lay person and should only be carried out by a veterinary surgeon in sterile conditions. I cannot but feel that unless the operation is necessary for medical reasons – the bitch has sustained a severe fracture of the pelvis or is a victim of that curious ailment sexual alopecia – the use of sexual or oestral suppressants is preferable to a surgical operation.

The fact that any surgical operation involves some risk to the animal certainly colours my opinion but it is the finality of the operation which is most disturbing, particularly as the operation is conducted when the bitch puppy is a mite of eight or ten weeks of age and it is also impossible at this age to detect if the bitch in question is going to grow into a mature animal which would make an ideal or exceptional brood. Despite my own feelings about neutering dogs and bitches one has to admit that each year sees more and more stock keepers neutering perfectly healthy, pyometra free bitches and castrating many young male dogs simply to prevent any inconvenience the sexuality of these animals might cause. The operations certainly prevent the spate of unwanted, unplanned litters of crossbred puppies that once filled the animal shelters of Great Britain.

Once a bitch has come into season for the first time she may be expected to come on heat every six or so months until her dotage and I shall deal with the duration of the period the bitch is receptive to dogs in the following chapter. Some bitches will come into season every nine or so months, while others become sexually receptive to dogs only once a year and once again I cannot resist an anecdote which shows just how easily the course of normal physical development can be diverted, even unintentionally. I keep, breed and train a very inbred strain of lurcher, members of which are not merely physically very similar, but have common psychological and physiological peculiarities. Some eight generations ago I was favoured by the birth of an exceptional bitch puppy who was all I desired and with whom I achieved such reciprocity that I could ask for no more from any dog. She came into season twice in her life and both times I bred from her mating the progeny to each other and to the brother of my brood bitch. My present lurchers are all descended from her and, I believe because of the in-breeding programme I practised, seldom come into season more than four times in their entire lives. They live to a great age – I buried a twenty-seven-year-old matriarch a few years ago – but because of a purely unintentional selection programme I have produced a strain of lurchers which can scarcely be called fecund.

Most bitches cease to come into season when obvious signs of approaching senility begin to manifest themselves. The Kennel Club suggest – indeed they insist – that no bitch over the age of eight years should be used for breeding, though many bitches will come into season when they are much older than eight years. Once more I must resort to the use of an anecdote to illustrate a point. When my oldest lurcher bitch, Fathom, was approaching twenty years of age – and both lurchers and greyhounds will live to great ages if allowed to do so, though sadly few are allowed to live out their life spans – I took to kennelling her with convenient kennel partners, for I was confident that her very obvious senility (she was virtually blind, almost deaf and very uncertain on her legs) also meant she was no longer fertile or likely to come into season. Finally I kennelled her with her grandson, a reluctant stud dog and an animal which had been crippled in a car accident. It was foolish but I was remiss about checking her for signs of approaching season and merely released both the cripple and the geriatric out for exercise each day. Fathom was five weeks pregnant before I was certain of her condition and far to long in whelp for me to get the misalliance annulled (a singularly inappropriate scientific expression, I've always thought). Thus I waited with some trepidation for the litter to be born. Fathom produced four healthy bitches with great ease and reared the litter with little effort. One of them became the best bitch I have ever owned. No doubt Kennel Club officials may have considered taking some form of disciplinary action against me for breeding from such a 'sere and yellow leaf' but fortunately lurchers as a breed type are not eligible for Kennel Club recognition. Nevertheless, I consider that the Kennel Club is correct and that a brood bitch on reaching the age of eight is a shade long in the tooth for motherhood.

However, I have perhaps discussed too long how to prevent a bitch from conceiving, how to neuter and annul the effects of mating, so perhaps at this stage it is expedient to counter-balance such negative advice and mention the subject of breeding a litter of puppies.

The Mating and Breeding of Dogs

Before the dog owner actually engages in the process of breeding a litter of puppies he or she would do well to question their motives behind producing such whelps.

Most dog breeders embark on such a project simply to experience fun, entertainment or merely interest from the project and frankly there is little to beat rearing a litter, watching the puppies develop different characters and traits for entertainment. On the debit side the rearing of a litter can be very restricting, very expensive, extremely time consuming and sometimes very distressing.

Other owners are keen to produce a replacement for a much loved bitch which they know in time will die and hence such breeders wish to continue a canine family which has qualities the would-be breeder considers desirable and worth perpetuating. This is the only reason I continue the family of lurchers I own, work and sometimes breed, despite the fact that, as I have explained, the bitches come into season so irregularly.

There is of course some money to be made from breeding dogs – many kennel owners succeed in making a living, albeit a hard-earned living, from producing a succession of puppies, but the profit margin from the sale of each puppy is usually quite small and it is by no means easy to sell puppies at certain times of the year, or to sell puppies of certain breeds of dog. Furthermore, the public's taste in dogs is a fickle one – one year there may be a great interest in German shepherd dog puppies while the next it may be impossible to sell these dogs, for spaniels or terriers may be in favour.

The homing of such puppies as the family bitch produces should be of prime consideration to the breeder, however, for the cup of the breed rescue societies surely runneth over and the kennels at these establishments are often packed with confused, ill trained, misunderstood animals who were sold or given to unsuitable owners. Prior to the bitch's conception friends of the owner will usually express a strong desire to obtain a puppy similar to the dam, but once the time arrives for a litter to be 'homed' such friends will often offer excuses for why they are unable to take a puppy. It is all too common a scenario to see the proud owner of a very rotund bitch confidently announcing that he or she has potential homes for a dozen or so puppies, only to hear the piteous bleat of the same owner some eight weeks or so later lamenting the fact that he or she cannot find homes for the whelps.

I have already explained that the popularly held notion that a bitch should produce at least one litter in her life to remain healthy is a fallacy. Hence I will not dwell on the subject further. However I urge dog owners with much beloved pet bitches to think very hard before considering mating their bitch and producing a litter of puppies, some of which may finish their days in breed rescue society kennels and may come to know a score of homes during their short lifetimes.

However, let us assume that the reader owns a bitch which has sterling qualities and as she ages the breeder wishes to produce a male or female puppy to replace this paragon. Once again, a word of warning must be given to the would be breeder – few puppies bred from paragons achieve the owner's affection and admiration in the same way as had the dam, until that is, the dam dies, after which the son or daughter of the paragon will improve dramatically and its true value be appreciated. Puppies tend to live in the shadow of illustrious parents, for while comparisons are odious, they are nevertheless normal where the performance of bitch and her offspring are concerned. The familiar bleat 'there'll never be another like Old Sal, Old Jen, Old Jill' and so on, is always to be heard when a dog owner compares a bitch to her progeny.

I confess to being as guilty as the next man where such comparisons are concerned. I own such a paragon, a lurcher bitch I call Merab, and until a week ago I believed her granddaughter, a look-alike bitch called Phaedra, to be a vastly inferior animal. A week and a half before writing this passage Merab skinned her front pads running over gravel grit – an extremely painful injury that incapacitated Merab and induced me to work the younger bitch alone and without the aid of her grandmother. Phaedra's ability seemed to improve at a startling rate and I have little doubt about her intelligence despite the fact that a month ago I regarded her as a dunderhead with little ability. So let me assume that the owner seeks to ignore the caveats hitherto mentioned and decides to breed from his bitch. Let us now follow the breeding cycle from preconception to parturition and attempt to explain the myriad peculiarities bitches and dogs are prone to manifest – and I repeat breeding a litter is a fascinating if very tying interest.

Firstly the decision to breed from a bitch should not be taken lightly nor embarked upon casually. The time to start considering the production of puppies is in fact as soon as a bitch comes out of her last season, some six months or so before the mating is to be attempted. This period of time allows the owner of the bitch to check the pedigree of the potential brood, seek out a suitably bred stud dog, and condition the bitch prior to mating. The six months also allows the would-be breeder to prepare whelping quarters and calculate how much food a growing litter is likely to consume – and possibly a chance to reject the notion of breeding from the bitch.

A bitch just coming out of season has deposited a layer of fat around her vital organs in preparation for the litter it possibly is about to produce, so a period of slightly restrictive feeding should follow the cessation of oestrus. One of the earliest dictums dog breeders seem to learn is 'fit does not mean fat' – though likewise fit does not mean emaciated, despite Metcalf's observations on how a species may seek to perpetuate itself at the expense of the individual. Once the oestrus has ceased the weight of the bitch can be slightly reduced by judicious deprivation of food. Serious exercise should follow this weight reduction and not precede it – the reader may care to remember the NGRC rules governing the racing and coursing of in-season bitches.

A would-be brood bitch needs to be exercised but not run to a state of exhaustion each day, or subjected to endurance feats that would test the mettle of a marathon runner. Yet a potential brood must be fairly lean if she is to be at her best at the time when she is mated, so the notion that one should obtain a litter from Old So So (a favourite and reliable bitch) as she is beginning to look a bit old, is certainly an unscientific and possibly dangerous idea. There is little doubt a slightly lean bitch (not an undernourished bitch) will breed not only a bigger litter but also experience less trouble whelping than an obese bitch. It can be quite dangerous for an obese bitch to produce a litter.

Next the breeder must unfurl that sometimes useless scrap of paper, kept only to impress the uninitiated, known as a 'pedigree' and attempt to ascertain details of the ancestors of the bitch and of the dog to which its breeder is considering mating the bitch. If the litter is to be produced for exhibition purposes, rather than as pets, the incidence of champions in the pedigree is obviously important for, to a certain extent at least, like tend to beget like. What is more important, however, are the inherited defects dogs and bitches appearing on the two pedigrees are known to manifest. For instance, I should be reluctant to breed from a pair of German shepherd dogs when both pedigrees manifested a high incidence of epileptics. Likewise it would be unwise to breed from two Bedlington terriers if many of the ancestors of the potential puppies were known to be carriers of copper toxicosis, or from the giant breeds (I have explained this expression earlier in the book) if there was a high incidence of hip dysplasia in the ancestors of both the dog and the bitch. A talk with a knowledgeable and reputable breeder of the breed in question is essential and it is wise to heed his or her advice regarding the choice of mate for one's bitch, no matter how conveniently situated a dog of the same breed may be.

Inbreeding, the act of mating closely related stock together, is neither a good nor a bad practice, for the results are determined by the quality of the stock featured in the pedigrees of either parent of the would-be litter. If there is a common denominator in both pedigrees that is known to be relatively free of inherited defects then by all means inbreed to this dog, providing he is of good type and disposition and does not breed defective puppies. If the common denominator is known to carry lethal or crippling defects – copper toxicosis, epilepsy or hip dysplasia – it would be wise to seek a stud where the influence of the undesirable ancestor will be minimal.

So, one assumes that the services of a suitable dog have been arranged and done so some weeks before the actual mating, one must add, for the majority of bitches seem to come into season during the spring and summer of the year and many of the best, most fashionable stud dogs may be in great demand at these times, even possibly over-booked.

Few owners of stud dogs expect the owner of the bitch to predict the exact day when she will be ready to conceive three or so months in advance of the mating, but it is very bad practice for the owner of the bitch to simply turn up without prior warning and expect the services of the stud dog.

The practice of taking the bitch to the dog's premises to mate and not vice versa is good sense. A dog that behaves like London's dominant primordial beast on its own premises may be decidedly uncertain of itself on unfamiliar territory. Some may make half-hearted attempts at serving the bitch, while others may become deterred by the slight initial hostility a maiden bitch may display towards an amorous male. Yet the same dog, faced with the self-same problems on his own territory, may not be deterred in the slightest and even mate with quite hostile, antipathetic bitches.

So to the actual process of mating of dog and bitch. Bitches which are bleeding or shedding heavily are very reluctant and unwilling to accept the attentions of a male dog. Indeed, most mature, well experienced stud dogs show a marked indifference to bitches in this condition – though many young, inexperienced stud dogs become excited by the presence of a bitch which is shedding heavily and will attempt to mount her. There is some considerable evidence to suggest that a mating which follows the elaborate courtship ritual favoured by domesticated and wild dogs is usually more successful than the forced mating insisted on by some owners of valuable stud dogs who are anxious to see their dogs come to no harm while mating. It must be added that an in-season greyhound bitch allowed to run free with a valuable but inexperienced young stud dog will sometimes cause him great hurt if he attempts to mount her.

There are many ways of detecting if a bitch is ready to stand for mating and will willingly accept the services of a stud dog and, while it is partly true that the majority of bitches will bleed for perhaps between five to ten days and then accept the services of a stud dog, there are no infallible rules concerning exactly when a bitch will stand for mating. The dog breeder can, however, undertake certain tests to determine the readiness of the bitch to accept the dog. If the handler stands over the bitch, facing her tail, and runs his hands down the flanks of the bitch, the in-season bitch which is ready to mate will usually turn her tail to the side and thrust her vulva outwards as if to invite the services of a male.

Some kennels resort to keeping a 'teaser dog', a male which while it is unsuitable for breeding is able to ascertain when a bitch is ready to stand for mating. Such a dog is allowed to engage in the elaborate foreplay that precedes mating but is not allowed to serve the bitch. A good teaser dog is however able to detect the readiness of a bitch to the day and while to allow such a dog to engage in the courtship ritual but not serve the bitch may be considered a shade cruel, such males are invaluable to any kennel, particularly if these teaser males are vasectomised to prevent any chance of a misalliance. However, even such seemingly invaluable assets to dog breeding have their limitations. Certain bitches will often display a great readiness to mate with a dog of their own choosing on their own territory, yet disdain the advances of another stud dog in the vicinity of his own kennels. I believe I mentioned that dog breeding can often be a heartbreaking venture!

The majority of dog breeding books, or even breed books which touch lightly on the subject of dog breeding, suggest that the bitch's oestral cycle follows a fairly rigid programme. Leedham (1962) suggests that the cycle can be divided into several distinct periods, starting with the swelling of the vagina which takes from five to seven days. During the first day there is a bright red discharge from the bitch's genitalia, which usually changes to a pale pink colour by the ninth day of season. When the discharge has lost what dog breeders commonly refer to as 'colour', the bitch will usually stand for the dog to serve her, though Leedham considers that ovulation begins only on the eleventh day of the cycle. It is certain that for the next four days bitches are most receptive to the attentions of dogs and conception is most likely during this period. Some bitches will continue to stand until the twenty-first day of the heat but the majority will reject the attentions of the male after the sixteenth day of the season – though bitches which are force mated (held and muzzled while the dog mates them) will often conceive if mated on the sixteenth day of the season. It is popularly believed amongst dog breeders that if a bitch is mated when only slightly receptive to the attentions of the male she will conceive a larger litter, but there seems little scientific evidence to substantiate this notion and by the twenty-first day of the season most breeders consider the heat to be over.

Let us therefore assume that the owner of the bitch had decided to breed a litter (and face the problems previously described) and taken the bitch to the premises where the stud dog resides. Should the bitch be unwilling to mate she will indicate this in no uncertain manner. Should the dog attempt to sniff at her genitalia she may spin around and face him, sometimes with a hostile expression on her face but, if she is prepared to encourage the advances of the male, wagging her tail. Some bitches simply sit in order to discontinue the courtship ritual and while an experienced stud dog is usually deterred by such a negative attitude, young inexperienced stud dogs will often attempt to mount the bitch and even mount her head, despite her unresponsive attitude.

A receptive female, a bitch which is ready for mating, will allow the male to explore her face, her anus and her genitalia though she may attempt to engage the male in a romp which precedes the actual mating. This romp, this canine foreplay, should not only be allowed but encouraged if, that is, the owner of the stud dog is willing to allow this play ritual – many owners of stud dogs are unwilling to allow this ritual for fear of damaging a valuable stud dog.

A fascinating courtship is now to be enacted if the bitch is ready to receive the male and frankly certain parts of this ritual defy explanation. The dog may now place his chin on the female's back and attempt to mount the female, clasping her around her 'waist' while executing a series of pelvic thrusts. Immature stud dogs excited by the scent and sight of the bitch may attempt to mount the female's head, but this is simply an indication that the male is immature or sexually over-excited and he will usually assume the correct mating position presently.

Once an experienced male has assumed the correct mating position he will usually execute a series of pelvic thrusts in an effort to insert his penis into the bitch's vulva. It may take several attempts for the male to achieve this penetration, but once the male has inserted his penis the frequency of the pelvic thrusts increases and the male's hind legs may leave the ground as he penetrates the bitch, though he may clasp the bitch's waist the tighter as he does so. At this stage the dog's hind legs may display what is known as a treading action as he seeks to ensure his penis is firmly in position inside the bitch's vagina. To date the mating ritual is little different from the behaviour of most other mammals and will not surprise the tyro dog breeder in the slightest. What follows however is an amazing sequence of events the reasons for which have defied explanations from veterinarians and behaviourists alike for centuries.

The next stage of mating is known by the somewhat grandiose expression as the behaviour of intromission – which I intend to explain more simply. The paddling action of the dog's feet may continue for a few seconds and he may visibly twist his lower regions as he continues to penetrate the bitch.

During this process the prepuce or foreskin covering the dog's penis is pushed back until the bulbous swelling of the dog's penis is pushed inside the bitch's vagina whereupon the bulb becomes considerably enlarged. The bulb is held even more tightly inside the bitch by the constrictor muscles of the vagina and at this stage the bitch may experience some pain and considerable panic. Some bitches thrash round wildly and may scream and even roll on the ground at this stage and wise owners of stud dogs usually insist the bitch is held during this stage of the mating to prevent damage to the male.

Breeders of powerful dogs or sight hounds which can inflict serious bites usually insist that the bitch is muzzled before the actual process of mating begins, to prevent damage not only to the stud dog but also the handler attempting to hold the bitch. I confess I have been savaged many times by terrified bitches which are in the process of being mated and I am now reluctant to assist the mating of an unmuzzled large, hard biting bitch. Some stud dogs have been terribly damaged by the cavorting of bitches with which they are attempting to tie. Hence few owners of stud dogs will allow what is euphemistically referred to as 'a natural mating' where a bitch is allowed to roll in agony once the bulb of the dog's penis swells within her. It can be argued that there is also a huge number of ruptured male street curs.

Once firmly locked (or tied) within the bitch the male will usually drop both his forelegs to one side of her and then rather awkwardly lift one hind leg over the bitch, so that the couple are standing back to back, resembling those rather obscene magnetically attached metal dogs that were sold in some number to the public during the opening of the Eiffel Tower, for the French are apparently fascinated by what they consider slightly bizarre sexual behaviour.

The strength of the 'tie', the locking of the constrictor muscles of the vagina on the bulb of the dog's penis, is little short of incredible and it usually requires a powerful shock to break the union. If the French are fascinated by the sexual behaviour of animals, the British are apparently nauseated by the spectacle, for a tie between two street curs in Britain usually triggers a race amongst housewives to fill pails of water to cast over the copulating dogs in order to break the tie. Apparently the sexual acts of animals should be performed in private this side of the Channel, but the sudden shock of both participants being doused in cold water usually does succeed in breaking the tie, although the chances are that by the time the cold water has been applied to the pair the dog will probably have succeeded in impregnating the bitch.

If not interrupted by the pails of cold water cast by prudish housewives the tie itself will last for perhaps half an hour, though there are reports of giant breeds of dog tying for far longer than this. In fact I have known a maiden dog and bitch terrier couple tie for over two hours, though a tie of this duration is exceptional and incidentally, despite the duration of the tie, the union proved to be unsuccessful.

Of course the question must be asked why do dogs mate in this manner, and the mating habits of the canineae are quite unique in the animal kingdom. Early dog book writers suggested that the curious position adopted by the participants during the action of mating made them less vulnerable to attack for the pair were able to sport 'teeth at both ends', as Dunbar put it. Yet rival males will seldom attack a male once it has tied with the female and the notion that other hostile predatory species would find it difficult to surprise a tied pair which are totally captivated by each other's sexuality is too ludicrous even to contemplate.

The notion that the prolonged tie is necessary for the conception of puppies is also slightly ridiculous. When the tie is broken by a sudden shock – the traditional dousing with a bucket of water – bitches are quite often found to be in whelp or at least impregnated despite the short duration of the tie. Dunbar and Terrasse both mention that chow chows and some allied breeds seldom tie yet are no less fecund than any other breed of dog.

Research conducted at Hancock's kennel in Sutton Coldfield suggests yet another explanation. It appears that at certain stages of seminal injection the pH factor of the seminal fluid changes dramatically and it is possible that a lengthy tie may produce seminal fluid which may possibly reduce the incidence of undesirable organisms in the bitch's uterus and thereby increase the viability of the foeti, or at least the number of ova which may be fertilised. Many breeders agree with this notion that a womb relatively free of infection is likely to produce larger litters and possibly stronger, healthier puppies. Some breeders do in fact inject bitches with antibiotics such as amphicillin shortly before mating to reduce the number of undesirable organisms which may be harboured in the uterus.

However, as yet no one seems to have come up with an explanation which explains why dogs of most breeds tie. I feel it would be presumptuous of me to offer my theory as to why dogs assume this curious position while mating, so I shall leave the reader to form his or her conclusions about the phenomenon.

It is certainly well worth the tyro dog breeder's while to take his bitch to be mated to an experienced well-bred stud dog rather than to take her to an inferior dog of the same breeding that is more conveniently situated and whose stud fee is considerably less. Some stud dogs are so experienced that they are able to mate females which tower over them (though bitches are usually smaller than dogs of the same breed) and will ascend platforms or piles of stones constructed by stud dog owners in order to be so placed as to penetrate the bitches they are required to serve. Hancock, one of the world's largest dog breeders, owns dogs so experienced as to wait until Hancock has constructed a mating platform of the correct height before the stud dog even attempts to mount the bitch. Some show only a casual interest in the bitch until Hancock deems the platform to be ready. It is perhaps worth explaining that all Hancock's stud dogs are fairly small, collie or collie-greyhound hybrids, while the brood bitches are greyhounds most of which are much bigger than Hancock's stud dogs.

There is certainly evidence to suggest that the greater number of times a dog serves a bitch the greater the chance of the bitch conceiving and the popularly held notion that a bitch can be served too many times by a stud dog is both ludicrous and inaccurate. Many professional dog breeders allow a bitch to be served every day she will stand for mating, though this is a tedious, time consuming practise so most breeders encourage a stud dog to mate a bitch on alternate days until she becomes hostile to the dog's advances. Some stud dogs are so enamoured of certain bitches that, providing the participants are separated immediately after coition they will serve the same bitch many times during the course of a day, but there is little benefit to be obtained from such a practise.

If the bitch has ovulated and produced sound healthy ripe ova, fertilisation may occur within half an hour of mating. Ova seem to be able to remain viable for nearly a day, though sperm are capable of fertilising ova for four or so days after ejaculation. Once fertilised the ova become attached to the uterine wall by dint of a placenta – and there is absolutely no substance to the once popularly held notion that the right ovary produces a preponderance of ova which will grow into male puppies while the left ovary produces ova most of which will grow into bitches.

However, perhaps at this point it is expedient to discuss the subject of what is known in the dog world as mixed litters. In theory if ten different males serve a single bitch in rapid succession it is possible, though a shade unlikely, for the bitch to produce ten puppies each sired by a different male. I have thrice produced mixed litters, twice by design, for at one time I tended to reject many scientific theories until I personally tested them. At one time I mated a Jack Russell bitch to her brother, then to a black, smooth-coated fell and then a border terrier male, all within the course of an hour, for males seem particularly desirous of mating bitches which have just been served by another dog. I produced one Russell type male, two black bitches and a border terrier look-alike in the same litter. Later in 1993 I produced by accident a mixed litter of Lucas and Lucas terrier crossbreeds when a stud dog with a penchant for sexual acrobatics managed to mate a bitch through the bars of his kennel. I have never seen a tie wrought under these circumstances and find it almost impossible to imagine. Hence I am confident that a conventional tie is not always necessary to ensure conception.

I seem to spend much of my time debunking old wives' tales or acting as an iconoclast where what is sometimes termed 'country wisdom' is concerned, but the 'three weeks worming' dictum once regularly obeyed by gun-dog breeders has more than just a grain of truth in it. A bitch should be in prime condition when she is ready to be mated and free of both external and internal parasites. The modern notion concerning tapeworms seems to be that they enjoy a symbiotic rather than a parasitic relationship with the host but they are such loathsome creatures that I find their presence in the stools passed by my dogs offensive. It was ancient practise to worm and deflea (fleas are great carriers of worm eggs) some three weeks before the bitch came into season, some three weeks after mating and three weeks before parturition. Now while such a system must have developed when anthelmintics (substances which expel worms) were decidedly dangerous to use and caused the bitch not only to be ill, but often to abort if used too soon after mating or too close to parturition, I would heartily recommend such a treatment, despite the method's antiquity, for the fact is that modern anthelmintics are milder and seldom cause even a very pregnant bitch discomfort.

Defleaing before parturition is, however, absolutely essential as dogs often ingest fleas which are causing them irritation and hence become reinfected with tapeworms. I am inclined to believe that the modern practice of disregarding tapeworms until these creatures are causing the dog some distress, or are too numerous in the droppings, as an unwise one, despite some scientific evidence to the contrary.

A bitch which is pregnant will show little sign of her condition until five weeks after mating, though some breeders claim to be able to determine if a bitch is pregnant before that time. During the fifth week of pregnancy the bitch usually experiences a substantial weight gain resulting from deposits of subcutaneous and abdominal fat. One assumes that this build-up of body fat is simply a food storing mechanism adopted by wild bitches who might find hunting is less fruitful during the later stages of pregnancy when the bitch is heavy in whelp, but there is little doubt that a pregnant bitch makes more efficient use of the food she ingests. Hence it is not good policy to overfeed – the antique stockman's word for such a practise was to 'sweat' – a bitch during the first weeks of pregnancy. However, there is some evidence to suggest that during this time while the quantity of food should not be increased a recently mated bitch should be fed a diet rich in minerals and vitamins to ensure the proper development of her foeti. Overfeeding at any stage of pregnancy is a dangerous practice, however.

By the time a bitch is six weeks pregnant her condition will be obvious, her girth will have increased greatly and her nipples will have enlarged and are often swollen. By this stage in the pregnancy even the most inexperienced dog breeder will be able to detect if the bitch is in whelp and I can never understand tyro breeders who take bitches scarcely five weeks out of season to a veterinary surgeon to determine if the bitch is carrying a litter of puppies. If the bitch has misallied with an unsuitable dog it is far too late to have the misalliance annulled – an 'injection' will usually only nullify a mating up to forty-eight hours after the misalliance. If the bitch has been mated to a dog the breeder has decided should be the father of the litter, then in six or so weeks the state of the bitch can be ascertained even by an amateur. If it is not in whelp there is nothing the breeder can do to correct this situation until the bitch comes into season again and is mated by the stud dog. I have gazed in wonder at proud, first time breeders taking obviously pregnant bitches to a veterinary surgeon's practice to determine if the animal is actually in whelp and I shake my head in despair at the breeder who takes a bitch three weeks out of season to the practice to ascertain if the animal is likely to produce puppies. Even a veterinary surgeon who specialised in the breeding of small animals would be guessing at the condition of a bitch a mere three weeks out of season, even though such a veterinarian is skilled at the art of abdominal palpation.

It is good practice to cleanse a pregnant bitch of round worms when she is some six to seven weeks pregnant and, despite the fact that this is an age-old practice, there is ample scientific evidence that such a worming is advantageous to the development of the foeti. When a bitch is perhaps six and a half weeks pregnant certain hormonal changes within her body trigger the migration of round worm larvae, or perhaps alert them to the presence of fresh hosts within the bitch's uterus. The larvae then migrate across the placenta and infest the foeti within the womb. It is virtually impossible for the average kennel owner to produce puppies which are totally free of round worms, though I believe that one such litter has been produced under laboratory conditions. However, should the bitch be wormed during the seventh week of her pregnancy when the round worm larvae become active, some if not all the larvae will be voided in the bitch's excreta. Piperazine-based chemicals are usually ideal anthelmintics as they have a low toxicity and are unlikely to harm either the pregnant bitch or the foeti she is carrying. Puppies should be wormed with a similar substance when they are three and six weeks of age and breeders will note the considerable reduction in the numbers of these vile parasites voided by puppies if their dams have been wormed during the seventh week of pregnancy. As mentioned before, there is a school of thought that suggests tapeworms enjoy a symbiotic relationship with the dog, but as yet no anatomist has suggested that round worms benefit the health and development of the dog in any way.

The gestation period of a bitch is roughly sixty-three days though it is not abnormal to find many bitches of the smaller breeds such as terriers whelping five days earlier than this time. In the last few days of pregnancy significant changes in the shape of the bitch's abdomen become apparent – there is a shift in the bulk of the abdomen from just below the rib cage to her hind quarters.

At this stage a bitch may become restless and seek a den to bear her puppies in – I have explained my theories regarding this desire to nest in enclosed spaces earlier in the book – and from the fifty-sixth day after the bitch has been mated the breeder should be vigilant about the prospect of the bitch whelping. Most bitches are able to produce their puppies naturally but in the case of brachycephalic breeds such as bull dogs, and even Boston terriers and sadly miniature bull terriers, it is necessary to assist the birth of the puppies by a Caesarian section – not a particularly difficult operation but one which must be performed by a qualified veterinary surgeon.

How sad that breeders have sought to exaggerate the physical peculiarities of breed types which were once the most dynamic of dogs, and perhaps some of the most physically perfect, until they have produced what can only be described as canine blasphemies which are unable to enter the world without the aid of expert veterinary assistance!

The Interaction between Man and Dog

I have deliberately terminated the chapter concerning the breeding of dogs with the comment that during the period of domestication of the dog – a twenty or so thousand year symbiotic relationship – dramatic physical and mental changes have been wrought in the dog, some of which have not always been advantageous to the survival of the species.

I am constantly accused of quoting the works of Ash, Rawdon Lee and other Victorian and Edwardian writers, but many of these writers coined epigrams which were not only succinct and pithy but often gave a fairly good evaluation of the dogs and breeders of this age. Ash is credited with the creation of the aphorism 'There are no bad dogs; merely bad trainers' – one of the most often quoted statements in modern dog books – and perhaps, just perhaps, in Ash's times this statement would have been correct.

There is little doubt that the Victorian dog breeder's total ignorance of disinfectants, inoculation programmes, canine pathology and practical kennel management would have facilitated the Darwinian selection programme allowing only the strong, the fit and the mentally sound to survive. There is also little doubt that the Victorian dog keeper's passion for savage culling would have further assisted the survival of the fittest. John Tucker Edwardes, the sporting squire of SealyHam, Pembrokeshire, is reported to have put out terrier puppies at walk with various tenant farmers. Should, during one of Tucker Edwardes' infrequent visits to these tenant farmers, one of the puppies show the slightest nervousness Edwardes, who apparently took his shotgun wherever he went, promptly shot the mite, disregarding the tenant farmer's pleas for the life of the whelp – though I hasten to add I am uncertain of the authenticity of the tales related about John Tucker Edwardes.

Will Humphries, Lord of the Manor of Ratlinghope and Streton in the Dale, culled his English setters heavily should they manifest the slightest undesirable mental trait – despite the aesthetic qualities of the animal in question, for he viewed nervousness and worst of all gun shyness as intolerable anathema – and dealt with what he considered as his 'mistakes' promptly and finally.

I have already stated that the Kennel Club must not be blamed for the development of undesirable breed characteristics in certain breeds of dog but the blame must certainly be laid firmly at the doors of breeders who specialise in breeding stock for exhibition qualities, regardless of the mental and constitutional abnormalities the breed is manifesting. Indeed, it might be suggested that Ash's quote 'There are no bad dogs; merely bad trainers' can no longer be considered as strictly true.

It seems at this point essential to mention that most worrying example of pathologically disturbed behaviour in dogs known as 'Cocker rage', a peculiarity that seems to manifest itself in solid coloured (particularly red) cocker spaniels which apparently manifested these peculiarities in the early 1950s when newspapers made much of the odd behaviour of red solid coloured cocker spaniels. Some of these spaniels can be decidedly dangerous, more dangerous in fact than some of the pit bull terriers which sadly fell foul of that piece of legal lunacy known as the 1992 Dangerous Dogs Act. Some of these red cockers (and solid blacks descended from these red spaniels) are often perfectly amicable by day, but become decidedly peculiar towards the late afternoon, hiding under blankets, curling up in undersized boxes and not only hiding insignificant objects but displaying a propensity to defend these objects to the death. At one time I earned a pitiful living retraining difficult animals – usually sight hounds, the most misunderstood of dogs – but after my first venture with a difficult red cocker spaniel which when the room in which it found itself was illuminated by a bright light crawled into an impossibly small space behind the Rayburn cooker and savagely mauled anyone who approached it, I crossed red cocker spaniels off the list of dogs I was prepared to take for training. Should one of the modern behaviourists who specialise in the modification of canine behaviour seek to chide me for my reluctance and inability to take up the challenge of ameliorating such a dog's behaviour, might I remind such highly paid dog psychologists that, while they are required to explain the peculiarities manifested by some dogs and suggests ways of making the dog's behaviour more acceptable, of sublimating the dog's behaviour, so to speak, the trainer is required or expected to break the dog of its idiosyncrasies and return an entirely transformed, well trained dog to its owners in a matter of a few days, and at the cost of a few pounds.

Hence, while I applaud the efforts such psychologists make to correct certain mental peculiarities certain dogs manifest, I can understand trainers' reluctance to undertake to retrain such animals. In fact, I consider it morally reprehensible of breeders to produce animals which have a very good chance of developing mental or physical peculiarities – though the incidence of cocker rage amongst red cocker spaniels has lessened since the 1950s.

There is, however, some truth in Barbara Woodhouse's book *No Bad Dogs*, though the book generalises far to readily to be scientifically sound. A firm hand, but not a hand that is too firm one must add, on any puppy during the formative period of its life – up to perhaps six months of age – will prevent many of the problems people experience with older dogs, and frankly many, many dogs are an embarrassment to their owners. If attention is paid to the social behaviour and to the training of young puppies and care is taken not to allow the puppy to develop undesirable qualities during this period, I would not expect the grown dog to behave strangely.

So much responsibility must be laid at the door of the breeder: the breeder must take care not to breed from animals which are either mentally or physically unsound, nor breed from disturbed animals even if these dogs are very aesthetically pleasing. Also the breeder must attempt to match up the puppy with the potential buyer and if necessary refrain from selling certain people dogs. I crave the reader's indulgence for the spate of anecdotes which are to follow to illustrate the point I have made.

I have met would-be buyers (and I hasten to add refrained from selling a dog to these people) who would clearly make the life of a puppy a living hell, without deliberately setting out to be cruel to the animal. A woman who is clearly far too house proud and omits to ask about the needs of the whelp but rather enquires if the beast will shed its hair over the furnishings, should not be sold a dog of any breed, for under such conditions even the most obliging dog will instantly be labelled 'a problem pet'. Dogs will certainly not help the house look more tidy, nor will they contribute to the neat appearance of any abode and breeders should make the fact known to the potential purchaser of a pet.

Breeders are obliged to tell buyers of the peculiarities of certain breeds of dog and not eulogise over the good qualities an animal might display without mentioning some of the peculiarities of the breed. For instance, a breeder of Siberian huskies is morally obliged to tell a potential purchaser that the delightful woolly ball the owner is trying to sell will grow into a mature animal which is difficult to recall and has an unwholesome antipathy to sheep.

Breeders of large types of dog with a potential for displaying aggression towards human beings – and it is surprising how many of these breeds are predominantly black and tan in colour – German shepherd dogs, Rottweilers, Dobermanns, and so on, should be extra careful about matching a buyer with the correct puppy. A socially inadequate man should be dissuaded from buying an aggressive, dominant male puppy which will clearly gain dominance over its somewhat weak-willed owner. Alas, here is the rub. It is often the case that such a socially inadequate man will seek to buy a large, bold male dog to compensate for the would-be owner's character weakness.

Frankly, I avoid buying or keeping back bold, aggressive male puppies, possibly because I dislike the scrabble for dominance that may result from the ownership of such a dog. When I ran a terrier pack of sixty or so terriers I found that I seldom came into conflict with the bitches, but found dominant male terriers less easy to control. I cannot help but feel that the first rule of dog ownership should be the quote from Hamlet, 'to thine own self be true' and to examine one's real reasons for wanting to own a particular breed of dog. It is also the breeder's duty to inform the would-be buyer – as politely as possible – that he or she would not be a particularly good prospect for the ownership of certain dogs. I am blissfully aware that the ownership of a particularly dominant male saluki would be a little too much for me, yet I know of trainers, dare I say it, far less competent than I am, who would do better with the training of such an animal.

There is little doubt that the majority of problem dogs taken to canine psychologists or behaviourists are male and Mugford suggests that many of these dogs might improve if castrated, for Mugford attributes some of these undesirable traits manifested by certain male dogs to a super-abundance of a male hormone called testosterone. He mentions that stallions when castrated become far less difficult to handle and male pigs certainly become less of a problem when emasculated. I feel I cannot agree with Mugford's notions and they are certainly contrary to those of Dunbar, whom I mentioned earlier in the book. I would suggest that if these problem animals have developed peculiarities attributed to a surplus of testosterone, by the time these animals have acquired these undesirable characteristics it is virtually too late to correct these peculiarities by dint of castration. Mugford is certainly correct in as much as castrates are unlikely to be attacked by other entire male dogs and hence are less likely to become involved in fights, despite the fact that a castrate will defend itself fiercely if attacked. I had the opportunity of observing the reactions of my male terriers, which are very aggressive, in the presence of a castrate of the same breed whose owner was unwise enough to believe that castration was the answer to all problems caused by aggressive male dogs. The presence of the castrate in the pack precipitated an amazing number of fights simply because the sebaceous and anal glands secreted more feminine odours and this seemed to provoke the entire males to persistently mount the castrated animal, who seemed deeply offended by the outrage. Mugford, however, could be correct in his belief that if dogs are castrated before they acquire male characteristics, they will seldom retaliate if other males inflict the above described indignity on them.

I am decidedly sceptical about advising any dog owner on how to ameliorate the conduct of any dog which has shown a marked aggression to a human being – particularly if the attack was unprovoked, and few attacks on human beings are unprovoked, one should add. A dog which displays an inclination to attack human beings at the slightest provocation is a biological time bomb and if it is to be kept must be prevented from perpetuating these attacks by muzzling, though the attack of even a muzzled dog is terrifying, one must add. Various papers published by the University of Ohio suggest that such aggressive behaviour might be controlled, but not terminated, by administering a stimulant called D Amphetamine, but owning such a dog (even a dog which is restrained by medication) is extremely dangerous and frankly I feel there is only one course of action open to the owner of an ultra-hostile dog. Even quite small dogs are capable of inflicting savage wounds and the attack of a large, powerful dog such as a rottweiler sometimes results in the death of its victim.

At one time most dog training manuals seemed to suggest that if a pet was given sufficient exercise the tendency for it to bite would be reduced. Yet some dogs can be run to a state of exhaustion and still display a furious antipathy to human beings.

Perhaps at this point it is expedient to mention the subject of canine aggression or, to be more exact, the hostility some dogs show to members of their own species. Quite clearly some breeds have been deliberately bred to be antipathetic (what a delightful understatement in the light of a recent dog fighting incident which has received massive but inaccurate media coverage) to other dogs. The pit breeds, the bull terriers, the Staffordshires, the English and the American pit bull terriers, have been deliberately bred and encouraged to fight other dogs, but other breeds are often troublesome fighters – and I know from experience just how much of a nuisance aggressive dogs can be.

Terriers are invariably aggressive and more than willing to avenge any insult no matter how trivial a human owner may consider that insult to be. In hunt service circles there is in fact a saying concerning the housing of terriers, 'kennel three, bury one', for once animals of this nature are restricted by housing, and hence are unable to escape from an attacker, a serious fight will result in either terrible damage or death. Three or more terriers which have lived together in harmony for many years will quite suddenly engage in a three way battle and two will set together to kill the third dog. Hounds will often live together amicably – though kennel deaths through fighting are by no means unknown – but terriers are invariably poised on the brink of trouble, virtually waiting for a trigger point which will cause a fight to erupt.

At one time I taught with Dr R.L. Martin, who had a particular interest in battered wives and children who seem particularly prone to being bullied by other children. To be brief and not particularly accurate, many of these battered wives and equally damaged children drift from one beating to the next and are victimised by both sexual partners and children alike. Some women may experience relationships with several men, all of whom will abuse and hurt them. Many children will be so severely bullied by their classmates that their parents will move them to other schools where for a while the child will experience happiness and freedom from bullying. However, once this child has established himself in the structure of his new class or school, it is often the case that once again the dreadful bullying starts. Some children have been known to pass through several schools and to attract bullies in each establishment.

I have used the word attract only after some deliberation for it appears many battered wives attract unsuitable sexual partners and some children unintentionally attract or incite bullying from classmates. Such people are known to sociologists and police officers alike as PVS cases or persistent victim syndrome cases. Prisons are full of such people who need special protection to allow them to survive, such is the hostility they engender amongst other prisoners. Likewise the Armed Forces produce a spate of men who 'don't fit in' and it is often policy to discharge such people, rather than risk them being hurt, damaged or even killed by their barrack mates.

It is virtually impossible to say why these people are bullied. Neither can those who perpetrate the bullying explain why they are deliberately hostile to the victim. Possibly some body language, some affectation, some mannerism, some peculiar movement or possibly even some undiscernible body smell may trigger hostility towards the victim – I am inclined to believe that human beings are a lot more susceptible to the effect of pheromones than our race is prepared to admit.

PVS victims have been observed amongst packs of wild dogs. Males afflicted with this problem are ostracised and driven off, only to die of hunger when unable to enlist the services of the rest of the pack during hunts for food. Females too are treated badly by the rest of the pack and seldom succeed in rearing a litter of cubs. The cubs of the afflicted females may also be attacked by the rest of the pack, despite the fact that some arcane reasoning usually prevents adult members of the pack from attacking defenceless youngsters.

The same problem occurs amongst kennel dogs and a PVS-type dog balances on a tightrope between life and death amongst its kennel mates. All will seem hell bent on killing the hapless beast and a kennel manager must be observant and alert if the afflicted dog is not to be attacked or slain. Huntsmen who observe hounds being constantly bullied by the rest of the pack wrongly draught the victims to other packs – with disastrous consequences, for such hounds are also bullied by the members of the new pack or, and this is more likely, killed within days of their arrival at the new kennel.

What is even worse is the fact that a PVS-type dog actually precipitates kennel battles amongst other occupants of the kennels and this peculiarity is due to one or both of two factors:

(a) the shape, behaviour and scent of the victim provokes attacks on it and the death throes of an animal incite havoc in the kennels.

(b) the arrival of a newcomer of any sort to the kennels.

However to explain the latter phenomenon it is expedient to mention the findings of Sterniger (1950) and I crave the reader's indulgence for yet another digression to illustrate a point.

Sterniger experimented with a group of captive brown rats, allowing them to establish a colony in a compound, the dimensions of which measured 12 yards by 10 yards. For a while the newly introduced occupants milled around aimlessly, displaying fear of each other rather than hostility to one another, until that is the first male and female paired. The pair then set to with a vengeance killing the rest of the group, the female slaying the does while the male disposed of the terrified bucks. Then for a while at least peace and equilibrium existed in the colony.

The does reproduced with the rapidity of which only rats seem capable and their children coupled incestuously to produce further ratlings. The now aging grandparents acted out their roles as doting ones and permitted and apparently enjoyed outrageous liberties from the tiny grey ratlings. Squabbles were infrequent and serious battles noticeable by the absence – until, that is, Sterniger introduced a newcomer to the colony.

At first the denizens of the colony or extended family ignored the rat, who seemed little different from the rest of the group. They then scented the newcomer and realising the different scent bristled with fury before attacking the hapless creature, finally killing the wretch and devouring it.

Then to Sterniger's amazement the group became extremely quarrelsome, fighting with great fury for no apparent reason and, what was even more curious, bucks fought and killed does. It took a considerable time before peace, tranquillity and equilibrium returned to the colony once more.

Sterniger also found that when rats were taken from the colony and kept in cages for a few days so that their scent altered a little sometimes they too were attacked when they returned to the colony.

So what do Sterniger's experiments teach the dog owner? Well, quite simply, despite the fact that Sterniger considered such behaviour to be specific to rats, the same behaviour pattern will manifest itself in a house where two or more dogs are kept or in a kennel where many dogs are lodged.

If Virgil was correct about being mistrustful of Greeks bearing gifts, the dog owner must be particularly vigilant about allowing strange dogs to enter his household or kennels where a state of peaceful equilibrium exists amongst the dogs. Friends wishing to lodge a dog for the weekend should be gently persuaded to put their pets into a boarding kennels rather than leaving the dog with his 'friends'. One often hears of two dogs which have lived in perfect harmony for years engage in a frightful battle and forever after to be antagonistic to each other. The chances are that this furious fight was precipitated by a strange dog being brought to the premises and upsetting the equilibrium of the house or kennels.

It is quite dangerous to take away bitches to be mated, particularly if the bitch resides some time with the stud dog. On returning the chances are the bitch will have lost much of her house or kennel scent and furthermore be tainted with the aroma of the stud dog to which she has been served. Cats seem particularly hostile to a female which has returned from a mating even if the queen has spent only a short while at the stud's premises.

It can of course be argued that dog dealers who allow a great number of dogs to pass through their premises seldom experience the fights so described. It can, however, also be argued that dogs in a dog dealer's kennel seldom stay there long enough for them to be absorbed into any form of social structure. Hence bewildered animals mingle together, snapping at each other in the manner of Sterniger's rats perhaps, but seldom engage in fierce battles. A lull in a dog dealer's trade, or a coupling of the often unhappy residents of the kennels would produce somewhat different results however.

I'm not a particular fan of Dr Roger Mugford, though some of his quotes are both memorable and repeatable and I believe it would be impossible for me to train a dog to the standard I require using his methods, but some of his notions on the treatment of phobias amongst certain dogs are well worth mentioning – indeed his book *Dr Mugford's Casebook* makes interesting reading.

At the risk of sounding like the poet William Blake, the cause of some of the phobias manifested by some dogs is baffling. The majority of gun dog training books go to some lengths discussing gun shyness or the fear of loud and sudden noises and offer some advice on how to deal with the disorder. Most gun dog breeders have overcome the problem of possible gun shyness long before the whelps are ready to be sold on to their new homes simply by firing a cap pistol while a litter of hungry puppies are feeding. Thus, what might appear as a startling noise becomes, in true Pavlovian fashion, the precursor to a pleasurable experience, namely a good meal. To take a gun dog to the sporting field for the first time and to subject it to the barrage of gun fire is bad practise and likely to induce gun shyness in the best bred gun dogs – a gradual introduction to loud and sharp noises is certainly good practise.

Books concerning gun dogs written at the turn of the century suggest that a gun shy dog might (and the operative word is 'might') be cured of its problems by tying in a position where it will be exposed to the constant barrage of gun fire until the dog has been cured of its gun shyness or, as was often the case, fitted and died of shock – I witnessed a dog die of shock after such treatment in 1948. I was quite a young child at the time and horrified at the spectacle, but I am amazed to find that this method of curing a dog of irrational fears is once more in vogue amongst dog psychologists, though the procedure has reared its ugly head bearing the label 'flooding'.

In psychological terms the expression 'flooding' means exposing the patient (or victim, call the creature what you will) to the entity it fears in greater intensity than the creature is ever likely to encounter normally. Dogs which display a terrible dread of traffic might be chained on the roadside of the M25 or dogs which are afraid of horses (and I confess I share such a fear) might be locked in a horse box for several days with a fairly quiet gelding. This technique of breaking an animal of a phobia experienced a revival in popularity during the late 1970s, but has been condemned by many psychologists and psychiatrists alike as being a relic of the snake-pit therapy once practised in Bedlam. The success rate achieved by this method is terrifyingly low and there have been reports of many animals become deranged after such treatment.

Most applied psychologists favour a somewhat different technique to allow an animal to overcome certain phobias and this technique bears a staggering resemblance to a method used by medieval Arab falconers to 'man' haggard or wild caught falcons. The following description may well offend the sensitive reader and I would advise such a reader to eschew the following paragraphs. Arab falconers were wont to take freshly captured wild birds and sew their eyelids together with fine gut. The bird would then be set in the middle of a busy bazaar and each day the hawk or falcon allowed a little more light by slackening the thread 'sealing' the eyes until the bird became used to the bustle of the bazaar. Many of the wild hawks, the Shabbaz or the goshawk, were given a pellet of some opiate during the early days of such 'manning' to render the hawk tranquillised until it could be accustomed to the presence of busy human beings. At one time dozens of such hawks and falcons were manned in certain bazaars and sadly several died after being overdosed with some opiate such as laudanum.

Many of the 'dog psychologists' (there surely must be a more appropriate word for applied psychologists with an interest in dog behaviour problems) have clearly adopted the Arab hawk manning technique to allow a dog to overcome a particular phobia. Let us assume that the dog is terrified of traffic, so terrified that it panics when taken out into a typical busy street. The dog is then sedated quite heavily, but not heavily enough to render it unconscious, and in this stupefied state walked along the street where it once experienced panic. The dog is only remotely aware of the traffic passing by it and seldom experiences distress.

The following day the animal is tranquillised with a smaller amount of the drug and paraded along the same street, doped but less stupefied than it had been the previous day. In this way the dose is diminished each day until the dog is able to endure the traffic without the use of medication. This technique is popularly used in preference to 'flooding', where the results may be more rapid or dramatic but sometimes so traumatic that the dog becomes a terrified wreck.

It is quite a sad state of affairs that the majority of dog psychologists are sent dogs which refuse to come to hand when called – a discipline they should have mastered at twelve weeks of age or younger – and it can be very difficult to persuade a recalcitrant adult dog to come to hand when it has missed the initial training which would have instilled such a discipline. Professional dog trainers who specialise in the training of difficult dogs usually adopt the check line technique when dealing with such dogs. The Middle Eastern sight hound types – the saluki and the Afghan – are some of the most difficult dogs to call to hand once their owners have failed to teach whelps of these breeds the discipline of coming to hand when they are called.

To correct this problem dog handlers usually fit the dog to a long check line and call the dog by its name. Should it decide to ignore the command the check line is wound in slowly and the dog patted, praised and offered a food reward from the trainer's hands. Some trainers will deny the dog food for a day or so before attempting this training technique, only feeding the dog when it can be brought in to hand either by winding in the dog, or as the training programme continues by coming to hand once it is called. Once it has learned to experience a pleasant sensation when it comes to hand – food or effusive praise – the dog trainer can congratulate himself and perhaps contemplate allowing the dog to run free of its check line, rewarding it each time it comes to hand. As with the trainer of hawks, the dog handler who allows the dog its first day of liberty must keep the animal sharp set or hungry before its first day of being allowed to run free. I have undertaken the training of three saluki dogs which refused to come to hand and trained them by this method, though my first attempts at calling in a free-running sight hound are always conducted in enclosed spaces so that I am able to recover the hounds should they fail to respond to my commands – one must expect the worst if training a difficult Middle Eastern sight hound.

During the last twenty years there has been a move away from the training methods used by handlers such as Konrad Most, whose training methods relied almost exclusively on the notion that a dog will do virtually anything to avoid pain, though there is little doubt that Most was highly successful at training the delinquent dogs he was sent to train. However, few trainers of Most's ilk are prepared to accept the fact that all dogs are different and the training methods must be varied to suit individual dogs. Lorenz in *Man Meets Dog* comments on the curious anthropomorphic attitude of one of his neighbours. Two of Lorenz's German shepherd dogs/chow chow hybrids, Pygi and Stasi (Lorenz seemed very enthusiastic about creating a new breed using chow chow blood) attacked a Maltese terrier and Lorenz punished both, flogging the more exuberant and tough Pygi while giving her daughter, a less confident animal, a light slap. Indeed, the essence of training is the flexibility of the trainer, whatever the dog training methods the trainer seeks to adopt.

My successes in training my own animals have been due simply to the reciprocity I experience with my dogs and the fact that I enjoy being in their company as much as they seem to enjoy being with me. When dog training or simply owning a dog becomes a chore it is time to wonder if one should keep a dog.

I meet an amazing variety of dog owners ranging from those who keep dogs for a distinct purpose, to those who keep a dog to create an image, but I never fail to wonder at the fact that despite the evidence that the dog has enjoyed a symbiotic relationship with man for upwards of twenty thousand years the dog, its habits, its social codes, and its sexual behaviour still remain a mystery.